THE
BEGINNING
OF THE END

THE BEGINNING OF THE END

The Book of Revelation and End Time Prophecy

Allen Robinson

THE BEGINNING OF THE END
THE BOOK OF REVELATION AND END TIME PROPHECY

iUniverse books may be ordered through booksellers or by contacting:

iUniverse
1663 Liberty Drive
Bloomington, IN 47403
www.iuniverse.com
844-349-9409

ISBN: 978-1-6632-3772-9 (sc)
ISBN: 978-1-6632-3773-6 (e)

Print information available on the last page.

iUniverse rev. date: 03/30/2022

CONTENTS

INTRODUCTION

THE WORLD WILL SOON END. IN THE BLINK OF AN EYE, THE WHOLE world will be changed. Destruction will come upon the earth in a wave of terror. The way we do things today will disappear and sudden and utter destruction will take place on this earth. Millions will die and death will reign upon this earth. Are you prepared, or will you be left behind?

With so many people in this world wondering when the world will come to an end, there has never been a better time than to study the Book of Revelation.

Revelation is the story of the apocalypse, the ending of the world, as God begins to pour out His wrath upon the earth. Nothing will stop the utter destruction of this world and those who blaspheme His name. When will the destruction take place? Some think it will be years from now, but the honest truth is that it can happen at any minute. The Bible says, "the Lord will come as a thief in the night." A thief comes in the moments we least expect.

In this book, you will see the future foretold through the Apostle John, as God shows the predicted end of the world. Will it happen soon? It will happen sooner than you think. The Book of Revelation has said the end is coming and the warning signs are clear, the question is will you be prepared?

1

100 Seconds to Midnight

Have you ever wished you could know the future? If you could find out what the future held for your life, would you really want to know? What if your future told of your unexpected death, would you still want to know? The book of Revelation is the future foretold through the Apostle John. Scripture has predicted the end of the world, but will it happen sooner than you think.

The Doomsday Clock is a symbol that represents the likelihood of a man-made global catastrophe. Started in 1947 by the members of the Bulletin of the Atomic Scientists, the clock is a metaphor for threats to humanity from unchecked scientific and technical advances. The clock represents the hypothetical global catastrophe at midnight. Imagine as if you watch the hands on a clock. The second hand slowly ticks second by second as you get closer to the global catastrophe. Scientists try to tell us that if we do not change the way we do things, the environment will be depleted and we will all fall into ruins. Even now there is a bigger push than ever for environmentally friendly products that will save our earth. No matter how much we try to save the world, this world is coming to an end.

You may say, "how can you say that?" God has said it, it's predicted. Nothing we try to do will save this earth from its coming end.

How can I be so sure? It is found in the book of Revelation. How long do we have? No one knows, but we can be sure that it will happen because we know that the Bible is true. The book of Revelation, written in 60 A.D. by the Apostle John gives us a detailed description of the destruction of this world.

> 2 Timothy 3:1-5 "But realize this, that in the last days difficult times will come. 2 For people will be lovers of self, lovers of money, boastful, arrogant, slanderers, disobedient to parents, ungrateful, unholy, 3 unloving, irreconcilable, malicious gossips, without self-control, brutal, haters of good, 4 treacherous, reckless, conceited, lovers of pleasure rather than lovers of God, 5 holding to a form of godliness although they have denied its power; avoid such people as these."

If you look at our society and the way it is going, this time has come and it is worsening! Matthew told us in Matthew 24 that the time will come when the Lord will return unexpectedly, taking believers to be with Him, before the coming of the days of wrath as God tears this world apart.

Matthew 24:37-39 "For the coming of the Son of Man will be just like the days of Noah. 38 For as in those days before the flood they were eating and drinking, marrying and giving in marriage, until the day that Noah entered the ark, 39 and they did not understand until the flood came and took them all away; so will the coming of the Son of Man be."

Just as in Noah's time the flood came without expectation bringing the ruin of all those who lived on this world besides Noah and his family. Look around you. People's conduct is changing for the worse. More authority figures are sounding the alarm that human nature is running wild and conditions are exploding out of control. No reasonable person can disagree with all the facts we have before us. Disorder, corruption, sickness, and famine already plaque the world we live in, and it seems nothing will get any better.

Many of the signs we see are terrifying and dreadful. Jesus warned that the earth will experience great turmoil, wickedness, war, and suffering.

Even now as Russia has invaded Ukraine in an act of war, President Putin has ordered that Russian nuclear weapons stand at increased readiness to launch, ratcheted up tensions with Europe and the United States and revived dormant fears from the Cold War era.

Matthew 24:4-8 "And Jesus answered and said to them, "See to it that no one misleads you. 5 For many will come in My name, saying, 'I am the Christ,' and they will mislead many people. 6 And you will be hearing of wars and rumors of wars. See that you are not alarmed, for those things must take place, but that is not yet the end. 7 For nation will rise against nation, and kingdom against kingdom, and there will be famines and earthquakes in various places. 8 But all these things are merely the beginning of birth pains."

All of these are not signs of the return of Jesus Christ, but things that will occur as the times get closer to His return. We have seen a drastic change as a society from a foundational stand upon God's Word to one which accepts every false doctrine and belief that one considers true. We have gotten away from the worship of God and began to worship false idols that we place before God. How much longer will God deal with the sins of this world and of the people who live on it? Many of these signs are being fulfilled. Wickedness is everywhere. Nations are constantly at war. Earthquakes and other calamities are occurring. Many people now suffer from devastating storms, drought, hunger, and diseases. We can be certain that these calamities will become more severe before the Lord comes. The reason that God gave us all these prophecies is so that we would not have to live in fear of these things, but rather be prepared and living in expectation of Christ's return

2

THE MISSING

IMAGINE THAT IT IS A NORMAL DAY IN YOUR LIFE. YOU ARE DOING YOUR normal activities: going to work, walking the dog, browsing on your computer, or enjoying your morning cup of coffee. When in an instant, the whole world changes. Imagine that you are at work and several people in your office have now suddenly disappeared. There is nothing left of them, but a pile of clothes lying on their chairs. Your co-workers suddenly look around as if some huge office prank has just occurred. They start laughing and cracking jokes about the clothes lying on the floor, while others are heard screaming as those they had just been talking to have just disappeared. Utter chaos has broken out all around you. Interruptions of the television news broadcast, stream across the television and computer screens with breaking news of missing administration and congressional representatives have disappeared. News reports of major traffic accidents are occurring around your area with news of missing drivers. There are reports of planes plummeting to the earth, causing instantaneous death for all those aboard the planes. You reach for your cell phone to try and contact your loved ones, but the line is busy. Your run to the office windows and see piles of cars stacked on top of each other, with flames pouring from the vehicles.

You can see smoke in the distance from planes that have now crashed into the buildings. There you stand afraid, worried, and helpless. You have been left behind.

Jesus promised that He would return to Earth to take His people to be with Him. He said in, John 14:1-3 "Do not let your heart be troubled; believe in God, believe also in Me. 2 In My Father's house are many rooms; if that were not so, I would have told you, because I am going there to prepare a place for you. 3 And if I go and prepare a place for you, I am coming again and will take you to Myself, so that where I am, there you also will be."

Are we living in the last days? Non-Christians will find it hard to believe that we are living in the last days of earth's history, but as we see through scripture, it's foretold. Should this cause us to fear? Should we dread the moments when the world will be destroyed? Not at all. The things we are about to see in the book of Revelation may scare you. The things that are about to come may make you afraid, but if you are a believer in Jesus Christ, there is no need to be afraid, because we will be saved from the terrible moments of what the Bible describes, which we call the rapture.

The rapture of the church is the event in which God "snatches away" all believers from the earth in order to make way for His righteous judgment to be poured out on the earth during the tribulation period.

If you look for the term rapture in the Bible, you will not see the word. The word rapture isn't used in the Bible, but the idea of the rapture occurs throughout the New Testament.

Luke 17:34-36 "I tell you, on that night there will be two in one bed; one will be taken and the other will be left. 35 There will be two women grinding at the same place; one will be taken and the other will be left. 36 Two men will be in the field; one will be taken and the other will be left."

The word we see in 1 Thessalonians 4:17 is the word Harpazó (har-pad'-zo) meaning to seize, catch up, snatch away. The word "rapture" "rapio" is the Latin for the two words "caught up" in 1 Thessalonians 4:17. At the time of Jesus' coming God will resurrect all believers who have died. They will be given new glorified bodies, and be taken from the earth, along with all living believers, who will also be given glorified bodies at that time. The rapture will involve an instantaneous transformation of our bodies to fit us for eternity.

The rapture is the time when Jesus comes back to gather those who have believed and trusted in Him as their Savior.

1 Thessalonians 4:16–17 "For the Lord Himself will descend from heaven with a shout, with the voice of the archangel and with the trumpet of God, and the dead in Christ will rise first. 17 Then we who are alive, who remain, will be caught up together with them in the clouds to meet the Lord in the air, and so we will always be with the Lord."

The Bible says that at the moment when Jesus returns for the believers it will be an instantaneous removal of all Christians from the earth.

> 1 Corinthians 15:51-52 "Behold, I am telling you a mystery; we will not all sleep, but we will all be changed, in a moment, in the twinkling of an eye, at the last trumpet; for the trumpet will sound, and the dead will be raised imperishable, and we will be changed."

Many have this idea that when the rapture does occur, we will gently float off this earth as if the gravity has been removed and we will fly up towards heaven to meet Jesus in the clouds.

The "twinkling of the eye" is the time it takes for light to enter the eye, reach the back of the eye, and be reflected back out. Light travels at 186,000 miles per second. To give a better understanding of this, humans blink at the speed of one second per blink. As we read in 2 Corinthians, the rapture will happen and we will be changed in the twinkling of an eye. The twinkling of an eye happens at the speed of eleven one-hundredths of a second.

This means at the moment you begin to blink before your eyelid has even started to close, eleven one-hundredths of a second has already occurred. To comprehend this, the rapture will have already occurred before we know it. It is instantaneous by our understanding.

When will the rapture take place? Nobody knows, only God knows. The return of Jesus Christ is likened to the coming of a thief in the night.

1 Thessalonians 5:2-6 "For you yourselves know full well that the day of the Lord is coming just like a thief in the night. 3While they are saying, "Peace and safety!" then sudden destruction will come upon them like labor pains upon a pregnant woman, and they will not escape. 4But you, brothers and sisters, are not in darkness, so that the day would overtake you like a thief; 5for you are all sons of light and sons of day. We are not of night nor of darkness; 6so then, let's not sleep as others do, but let's be alert and sober."

The key element of Jesus' comparison is that no one will know when He will return. Just as a thief catches a household by surprise, Jesus will catch the unbelieving world by surprise when He returns in judgment. The Bible says that no man knows the day, nor the hour, nor the time when Jesus will come, He comes like a thief in the night.

Why would they say Jesus comes like a thief in the night? When a thief comes in the night what happens? You are unprepared. It happens at a time you are not expecting. If you knew a thief was going to break into your house at a certain time, you would be prepared.

Many people throughout history have tried to determine when Jesus was coming back. They have used numbers, and depictions from the Bible to determine the exact moment he would return. Several years ago, there were many who were expecting Jesus to return. They posted big billboards on the side of the road, they handed out flyers, and they wrote books on the reason Jesus would return. But what happened? Jesus had not come back. Here is the reason why.

> Matthew 24:36–39 "But about that day and hour no one knows, not even the angels of heaven, nor the Son, but the Father alone. 37For the coming of the Son of Man will be just like the days of Noah. 38For as in those days before the flood they were eating and drinking, marrying and giving in marriage, until the day that Noah entered the ark, 39and they did not understand until the flood came and took them all away; so will the coming of the Son of Man be."

In 1988, Edgar Whisenant wrote a book called, "88 Reasons Why the Rapture Will be in 1988." What was the response to Whisenant's predictions? Thousands took the booklet seriously. Some even quit their jobs to prepare for the rapture and many pastors saw attendance in their churches increase. Many Christians shrugged the booklet off as being part of a huge sham. Others, though, while not accepting the specific predictions, praised the booklet for reminding them of the imminence of the rapture. But no man knows the day nor the hour.

Even today, our society has predicted the ending of the world. You may remember in 2012, when the Mayan calendar was predicted to end, people thought that the world would be destroyed. There was even a movie called, "2012", that showed the destruction of the earth.

In all the speculation here is one thing that we can be comforted with, we can find reassurance by replacing the anxiety of not knowing the day, with the expectation of that moment when it will happen. The rapture of the church, those who are believers in Jesus Christ, could happen at any moment. The key to having peace of the rapture is to replace anxiety of the present with the certainty of the future.

In the first three chapters of Revelation, we see mention of the church. Take notice that after those three chapters and before the tribulation begins, the church is not mentioned again. In Revelation 4, the Apostle John was brought into heaven. Could this be a symbol and sign that the church will be removed before these events take place?

> Revelation 3:10-11 "Because you have kept My word of perseverance, I also will keep you from the hour of the testing, that hour which is about to come upon the whole world, to test those who live on the earth. 11 I am coming quickly; hold firmly to what you have, so that no one will take your crown."

As Christians, we have been told that Jesus is going to come back and take us home. He is going to protect us from what is coming in the end times during the tribulation period on this Earth. Here is the certainty of the future that we hold as Christians, that by knowing Jesus Christ our Savior, He guarantees our future in a place prepared with Him.

There are many in this world today who claim that they hold the answer to the world's problems and that they can bring salvation. How many different religions are there that say there are numerous ways to heaven and that they have the way to heaven? How many religions promise that you can get to heaven based on your good works?

In 1997, there was a group of people who called themselves the Heaven's Gate religious organization. They believed in heaven, but their idea to get to heaven was that they had to wait for the aliens to come to get them.

In 1995, after discovering the comet Hale-Bopp, the Heaven's Gate members became convinced that an alien spacecraft was on its way to earth, hidden from human detection behind the comet. In 1997, the comet Hale-Bopp passed near Earth. In late March 1997, as Hale-Bopp reached its closest distance to Earth, thirty-nine members drank a lethal mixture of phenobarbital and vodka and then laid down to die, hoping to leave their bodily containers, enter the alien spacecraft, and pass-through Heaven's Gate into a higher existence.

There are many false religions in this world that say they know the way to get to heaven, but as the Bible says, there is only one way to get to heaven and that is through Jesus Christ.

> John 14:6 "Jesus said to him, "I am the way, and the truth, and the life; no one comes to the Father except through Me."

Jesus said, "I am the way." He didn't say follow a religion. Religion is made up of man-made rules in order to get to God. Religion states, you must do in order to be saved. What we have as Christians is called a relationship. We have been brought into a relationship with God through Jesus Christ. We do not have a religion with God, we have a relationship with God through Jesus Christ. Religion is man's way to get to God. Jesus said, "He is the way, the truth, and the life," and "no one comes to the Father except how through me."

Even with the good news of Jesus returning for us, many don't want Jesus to come back yet. Some have said to me, "I don't want Jesus to come back yet because I want to get married." "I want to have a good job first." "I want to have a house and a family." I want, I want, I want.

What we need to realize is that absolutely nothing in this world that could be better than what God has in store for us in eternity. Imagine for a moment, you're living in a cardboard box, in the dirt under a bridge. You hardly get anything to eat most days and someone comes along and says to you, "You don't have to live here anymore. I have a mansion for you and you can have everything you ever wanted. Every need you have or will ever need will be fulfilled and supplied to you. Everything you ever wished for is right here for you." You say to that person, "But I like my cardboard box, I like eating leftovers from the trash can." No, that will not happen. You long for the mansion. You will leave it all behind because you are going to a better place.

This is what it's like with Jesus Christ, He offers us everything if we just leave the old world and our sins behind. Compared to what Jesus Christ gives us, this world is horrible. Do you think this world has the best food you've ever eaten? It's a sinful and corrupt world. It's like eating garbage compared to heaven. Maybe you have been to some of the best places in the world where you are on a beach with the Sun and beautiful crystal-clear water. Everything in this world could be compared to garbage based on what God has in store for us.

How much longer can we stay here in our cardboard boxes and be comfortable? God says, "I have something so much better for you, and so great you can't even imagine what it's like." In heaven, we can't even imagine what it is going to be like because our minds can't understand it.

Jesus says, "I'm going to prepare a place for you and when I go, I will come again." When the rapture occurs, this is the moment that Jesus is going to come and take us home to heaven. It could happen at any time and at any moment. Literally, it can happen in 5 seconds. There's nothing that has to be done or completed for Jesus to come back. It could be in three seconds, one week or one month. Are you anticipating that moment?

> 1 Thessalonians 4:13-17 "But we do not want you to be uninformed, brothers and sisters, about those who are asleep, so that you will not grieve as indeed the rest of mankind do, who have no hope. 14 For if we believe that Jesus died and rose from the dead, so also God will bring with Him those who have fallen asleep through Jesus. 15 For we say this to you by the word of the Lord, that we who are alive and remain until the coming of the Lord will not precede those who have fallen asleep. 16 For the Lord Himself will descend from heaven with a shout, with the voice of the archangel and with the trumpet of God, and the dead in Christ will rise first. 17 Then we who are alive, who remain, will be caught up together with them in the clouds to meet the Lord in the air, and so we will always be with the Lord."

Not only will the rapture be a victory for living believers who are caught up to Christ, but also for all the believers who have died before the coming of the rapture.

As a pastor, one of my duties is to speak at funerals. When I speak to the family before the funeral, I ask one important question, "Did the person who passed away know Jesus as their Savior?" Because how a funeral is given is different for someone who knows Christ as their Savior versus someone who does not. For Christians, having put their trust in Jesus Christ makes a big difference. For people who pass away knowing Christ, they are at home in heaven with Christ.

Not that I am not sympathetic to those who are still left here on earth, but for a believer, it is a glorious day, it is a day of victory for them. Yes, we have lost someone who was with us, but this is not the end of the story. This may be a short goodbye until we are reunited with them in heaven. For the person who does not know Jesus Christ as their Savior, the person is in hell. There is no comfort for them. There is no glorious news of redemption. Only despair and pain. You cannot bring encouragement to the family of those who pass away without Christ, because their loved one is in hell burning forever and ever and ever with no end. There is no joyous occasion that we celebrate at the funeral of an unbeliever.

For believers, we do not grieve like the rest of mankind, who have no hope, because our hope is not found in our works, but in Christ Jesus. We have the answer. We have hope and, we have our travel plans arranged for heaven because of Jesus.

We who are still alive, who are left until the coming of the Lord, will not die. For the Lord will come down from heaven with a loud command and the voice of the archangel and with a trumpet call of God the dead in Christ will rise first. This means the bodies of those who perished will be reunited with their spirits and they will be with the Lord forever.

Let me explain to you the dichotomy of the human being. Our body is made up of two parts. We have a body, which everyone can see and we also have a spirit or a soul. Our spirit or our soul is where we find our mind and our will. This is how God created us. If I would die right now my body would be here. The moment that our body dies our spirit or our soul leaves the body and goes up to heaven. When the time comes for the rapture God reunites the spirit of those who have died, with their new bodies. God's plan was never for us to be just a spirit, but body and spirit as he originally created us. We will have better bodies that will never die. Not the ones we have now which are sinful and are decaying day-by-day.

Do you realize that the moment you were born, you start to die? As soon as we're born our cells start to die and break down. Why do you think as we get older that our bodies hurt more, our hair falls out, and our muscles grow weak? We all may have realized that we are not the same person we were when we were twenty-one years old. As I get older, I find I can't recover as fast as I used to. Our bodies are slowly breaking down.

Look at people who are 80 and 90 years old, are they still out on the football fields? Are they playing on the playgrounds like we used to do as children? No, because our bodies are breaking down. This is what happens in this sinful world.

At the trumpet call of God, which can happen at any moment, and at any second, we who are still alive will be caught up together with them in the clouds to meet the Lord in the air and we will be with the Lord forever. We will have new bodies and live in perfect conditions forever.

> 1 Corinthians 15:54-57 "But when this perishable puts on the imperishable, and this mortal puts on immortality, then will come about the saying that is written: "Death has been swallowed up in victory. 55 Where, O Death, is your victory? Where, O Death, is your sting?" 56 The sting of death is sin, and the power of sin is the Law; 57 but thanks be to God, who gives us the victory through our Lord Jesus Christ."

Back in the Old Testament times of the Bible, the Jewish people had an elaborate wedding ceremony that literally parallels the rapture of the church. In the traditional Jewish wedding, before the ceremony happens, the groom plans for the day of the wedding, but he does not tell the bride when he is coming to get her for the ceremony. The bride would not know when the groom was coming for her.

The bride had to be prepared at any moment. The bride would get up very up early in the morning, making herself ready, and then wait, with anticipation for the groom. He may come early in the morning or late in the afternoon, the bride had no idea. When the groom would get close to the bride's house, he would blow a ram's horn announcing the moment of his coming. The groom would then take the bride and go to his father's house for the wedding ceremony.

This is the same thing that happens with the rapture. The Church is the bride. We are to make ourselves ready and wait for the moment of Jesus' arrival. We do not know the day or the hour when Jesus is coming for us, but we need to be prepared. At the trumpet sound, the archangel will announce the coming of the King and Jesus will come to take us to His Father's house for that final unity of marriage where we, as the Church, the bride of Christ, will be with Him forever.

> Revelation 19:7-9 "Let's rejoice and be glad and give the glory to Him, because the marriage of the Lamb has come, and His bride has prepared herself." 8 It was given to her to clothe herself in fine linen, bright and clean; for the fine linen is the righteous acts of the saints.9 Then he *said to me, "Write: 'Blessed are those who are invited to the wedding feast of the Lamb.'"
> And he said to me, "These are the true words of God."

The believers in Jesus Christ are considered the bride of Christ. He will come back and take us to the Father's house, which is in heaven, to be with Him, forever in His presence. As the Church, we who have trusted Jesus as our Savior, are in the betrothal or engagement period waiting for the moment, when the horn sounds and Jesus comes back for us in the rapture. Will you be ready?

3

OVERWHELMED

NOW AS WE COME TO THE BOOK OF REVELATION, THE APOSTLE JOHN, who was imprisoned on an island called Patmos for preaching the Gospel of Christ, was given a vision by Christ. This vision that he was shown is what we will call the "beginning of the end."

Revelation 1:10-16 "I was in the Spirit on the Lord's Day, and I heard behind me a loud voice like the sound of a trumpet, 11 saying, "Write on a scroll what you see, and send it to the seven churches: to Ephesus, Smyrna, Pergamum, Thyatira, Sardis, Philadelphia, and Laodicea."12 Then I turned to see the voice that was speaking with me. And after turning I saw seven golden lampstands; 13 and in the middle of the lampstands I saw one like a son of man, clothed in a robe reaching to the feet, and wrapped around the chest with a golden sash. 14 His head and His hair were white like white wool, like snow; and His eyes were like a flame of fire. 15 His feet were like burnished bronze when it has been heated to a glow in a furnace, and His voice was like the sound of many waters.

16 In His right hand He held seven stars, and out of His mouth came a sharp two-edged sword; and His face was like the sun shining in its strength."

As John begins this moment of his journey, I imagine he is at a loss of words for the unspeakable glories of God, that now dance before his eyes. As John shares throughout the book of Revelation, he will attempt to describe everything he sees in intricate details. What you will find John using to describe his vision is what we call in the English language, a simile. A simile is a figure of speech that tries to compare one thing with another, such as; brave as a lion, or bright as the sun.

Something we must remember is that John is limited in the things that he has seen. For instance, John has never seen a missile flying through the sky or the advancements of the technology we have in our society today. John has never seen a skyscraper or a nuclear bomb. He does not know what an airplane is, or a car. What John will attempt to do is to give us a vivid description of the things that he has seen or knows from his lifetime.

Revelation 1:13-15 "I saw one like a son of man, clothed in a robe reaching to the feet, and wrapped around the chest with a golden sash. 14 His head and His hair were white like white wool, like snow; and His eyes were like a flame of fire. 15 His feet were like burnished bronze when it has been heated to a glow in a furnace, and His voice was like the sound of many waters."

As John looks upon this man, he does not see a man who has white hair like white wool. This is not an older man or a grey-headed man. What John sees is someone whose head and body are wrapped in glory appearing in white.

Even when we read in Luke 9, Peter, James, and John had seen the same experience when Jesus was on the mountain speaking with Moses and Elijah in the transfiguration. Jesus' appearance became different as His glory showed through Him.

> Luke 9:29 "And while He was praying, the appearance of His face became different, and His clothing became white and gleaming."

"His eyes were like fire." The man's eyes were not literally on fire, but His eyes had a piercing glow to them. It was as if the eyes of this man were able to see into a person's heart. "His feet were like burnished bronze when it has been heated to a glow in a furnace and His voice was like the sound of many waters."

John hears the voice of this man, which he attributes to rushing waters.

Have you ever been to Niagara Falls? Have you ever had the chance to stand on the boat or on the side at the waterfall? The rushing water has the sound of a roar. It pours over the falls with great power, strength, and might. As the rushing waters spill millions of gallons over the falls, the sound of the water can be deafening. Just like water, this voice that he heard was like the sound of rushing water. This voice was of one with power. It was intense.

His feet were as glowing bronze, like iron, steel, or gold that has been melted in a fiery furnace. His hands held the stars of the sky, and out of his mouth came a two-edged sword. This man did not literally have a sword coming out of His mouth, but the words that came out of the mouth were words that pierced his heart and soul. Words that were delivered with strength and power. This was the Word of God.

Hebrews 4:12 "For the word of God is living and active, and sharper than any two-edged sword, even penetrating as far as the division of soul and spirit, of both joints and marrow, and able to judge the thoughts and intentions of the heart."

Revelation 1:17-18 "When I saw Him, I fell at His feet like a dead man. And He placed His right hand on me, saying, "Do not be afraid; I am the first and the last, 18 and the living One; and I was dead, and behold, I am alive forevermore, and I have the keys of death and of Hades."

Who was this man? Who could have power such as this? It was none other than the King of Kings and the Lord of Lords, the Alpha and the Omega, the Beginning and the End, the Messiah, the Savior. It was Christ the Lord! When John realized who he was seeing, in an instant, he dropped with his face to the floor.

John had become so overwhelmed by the glory of Christ that he became limp and laid down in fear as a dead man.

Notice that John did not get down on one knee and just bow his head in reverence. He collapses in front of Jesus. John was so overwhelmed by the power of who he was seeing, and by the voice he was hearing, that at that moment it took his breath away. I am sure this terrified John. How could he see Jesus in all His glory and still live? It was at that moment when John, lying face down on the ground, suddenly felt the gentle, but strong hand of Jesus reached down and touch him. At that moment, that gentle, but powerful voice, which spoke creation into being said to John, "Do not be afraid; I am the first and the last, and the living One; and I was dead, and behold, I am alive forevermore, and I have the keys of death and of Hades." It was Jesus! The Son of God. How could he be so overwhelmed and so comforted at the same time? Because it was Jesus, his Savior.

4

THE THRONE ROOM
OF HEAVEN

HAVE YOU EVER SEEN A THRONE ROOM OF A KING OR QUEEN? TAKE FOR instance the throne room at Buckingham Palace. The throne room is decorated with high ceilings, majestic designs, and ornate décor that embellishes the room. Gold and silver, marble and granite, huge halls, and a central throne that would be fit for a king. We may stand in awe of the beauty of the king's throne room, but there is nothing that could compare to the throne room in heaven.

> Revelation 4:1-4 "After these things I looked, and behold, a door standing open in heaven, and the first voice which I had heard, like the sound of a trumpet speaking with me, said, "Come up here, and I will show you what must take place after these things." 2 Immediately I was in the Spirit; and behold, a throne was standing in heaven, and someone was sitting on the throne. 3 And He who was sitting was like a jasper stone and a sardius in appearance; and there was a rainbow around the throne, like an emerald in appearance. 4 Around the throne were twenty-four thrones; and upon

the thrones I saw twenty-four elders sitting, clothed in
white garments, and golden crowns on their heads."

John's imagination could never compare to what he saw before
his eyes. "Immediately I was in the Spirit, and behold, a throne was
standing in heaven, and someone was sitting on the throne. And He
who was sitting was like a jasper stone and a sardius in appearance; and
there was a rainbow around the throne, like an emerald in appearance."

The throne room showed brilliant realms of colors that inhabited
the center of heaven. Essences of light flowed from the throne as all the
colors of the rainbow weaved their way through and around the throne.

As John saw the throne, it took his breath away. There in the center
of heaven stood a throne, not one made by man, but one made for the
eternal Father. On the throne was not an old guy with a long beard, like
a grandpa figure, like most people like to think. It was not a huge man
sitting on the throne. The one who inhabited the throne was God the
Father. Not a God who was confined to a body, but the everlasting God.
The one who existed in the past, the present, and the future all at once.

Our minds have trouble thinking of God the Father as a Spirit.
John 4:24 says, "God is spirit, and those who worship Him must worship
in spirit and truth."

I think we try to confine God into human form, but God is Spirit.
The only part of the Godhead who we see as a man is Jesus Christ. God
understands that in our minds we tend to relate better to a human form.
Jesus is that representation of God to us. I think that knowing Jesus helps
us better relate to God because we see Him in a relationship as we are.

But we must realize that God is infinite. God does not need a body. God the Son came to earth in human form (John 1:1), but God the Father did not. Jesus is unique as Emmanuel, "God with us" (Matthew 1:23). Even though God is spirit, He is also a living, personal being. As such, we can know Him personally. God also has the basic characteristics of personality, intellect, emotions, and will. He thinks, He feels, and He acts. Because He is a living person, we can get to know Him personally and communicate with Him freely as we would with anybody else.

I just imagine John with his mouth open wide, standing in awe of God and His throne room as he tries to write everything that he sees. John is seeing the wonders of the majesty of the throne room. This is something his eyes have never seen or experienced before. The worship of a million angels singing with melodies and music so sweet, it penetrates John's heart to the core.

Everything is so beautiful and marvelous, so spectacular that his head was now spinning around in all directions, just trying to catch every brilliant color and sight that the throne room holds. Oh, and the smell. The air is so sweet, that breathing is like filling your mouth with the most savory desserts. His body was filled with joy and laughter that overwhelmed every sense in his body. His heart's desire was to join in the praise and worship, but also to laugh at the unspeakable joy that overfilled his soul. I'm sure as John stands there, lost in this one moment, it seems like a thousand years have passed.

John took special notice to those who sat on the thrones around God. There were twenty-four elders sitting on thrones, clothed in white garments, with golden crowns on their heads. The 24 elders with crowns upon their heads are the representation of the church. They are the body of believers who are there with God at the throne.

> James 1:12 "Blessed is a man who perseveres under trial; for once he has been approved, he will receive the crown of life which the Lord has promised to those who love Him."

> Revelation 2:10 "Do not fear what you are about to suffer. Behold, the devil is about to throw some of you into prison, so that you will be tested, and you will have tribulation for ten days. Be faithful until death, and I will give you the crown of life."

We are also told in scripture that believers will rule and reign with Christ.

> 2 Timothy 2:10-13 "For this reason, I endure all things for the sake of those who are chosen, so that they also may obtain the salvation which is in Christ Jesus and with it eternal glory. 11The statement is trustworthy: For if we died with Him, we will also live with Him; 12If we endure, we will also reign with Him; If we deny Him, He will also deny us;13If we are faithless, He remains faithful, for He cannot deny Himself."

Some people also have the misconception that when we get to heaven there will be a huge whiteboard that lists every one of our sins. This is the wrong type of thinking. When Christ died for our sins, he forgave every sin that we have done and every sin that we will ever do.

> Hebrews 8:12 "For I will be merciful towards their wrongdoings, and their sins I will no longer remember."

> Isaiah 43:25 "I, I alone, am the one who wipes out your wrongdoings for My own sake, And I will not remember your sins."

> Psalm 103:12 "As far as the east is from the west, So far has He removed our wrongdoings from us."

When believers get to heaven, we will all stand before the throne of God. Not for a time of judgment for our sins, but as a reward ceremony for our faith and trust in God.

> 2 Corinthians 5:10 "For we must all appear before the judgment seat of Christ, so that each one may receive compensation for his deeds done through the body, in accordance with what he has done, whether good or bad."

The judgment seat of Christ does not determine salvation; that was determined by Christ's sacrifice on our behalf when He died on the cross for us. We should not look at the judgment seat of Christ as God judging our sins, but rather as God rewarding us for our lives.

> John 5:24 "Truly, truly, I say to you, the one who hears My word, and believes Him who sent Me, has eternal life, and does not come into judgment, but has passed out of death into life."

In 2 Corinthians 5 the "judgment seat." is a translation of one Greek word, the word "bema". The bema is the reference to the Greek athletic contests like the Isthmian games or Olympic games.

Just as we participate in the Olympics today, the contestants would compete for the prize under the careful scrutiny of judges, who would make sure that every rule of the contest was obeyed. At the end of the event, the victor, who participated according to the rules and won, was led by the judge to the platform called the Bema. There, a laurel wreath, also referred to as a Bema Wreath, was placed on the head of the victor, as a symbol of victory. As believers, when we arrive in heaven, we will not stand on a judgment seat, as a convicted criminal stands before a courtroom to face criminal charges or judgment before God. We will stand on the Bema Seat to be rewarded for a life lived for God.

> Revelation 4:5-8 "Out from the throne came flashes of lightning and sounds and peals of thunder. And there were seven lamps of fire burning before the throne, which are the seven spirits of God; 6 and before the throne there was something like a sea of glass, like

crystal; and in the center and around the throne, four living creatures full of eyes in front and behind. 7 The first living creature was like a lion, the second creature like a calf, the third creature had a face like that of a man, and the fourth creature was like a flying eagle. 8 And the four living creatures, each one of them having six wings, are full of eyes around and within; and day and night they do not cease to say, "Holy, holy, holy is the Lord God, the Almighty, who was and who is and who is to come."

With the sound of the million angels lifting their voices in song, the echoing thunder, and the lighting that roared around the throne, all of this added to the amazement of John at seeing the power and majesty of God.

Even the strange creatures who stood before the throne of God left John in wonder. The creatures were something that John had never seen before. John noticed that these special angels had a specific part of worship. Their purpose has to do with declaring the holiness of God and leading in worship and adoration of Him and His name.

The word "holy" as defined in Merriam-Webster dictionary is "religious or morally good; exalted or worthy of complete devotion as one perfect in goodness and righteousness." (https://www.merriam-webster.com/dictionary/holy)

The Hebrew word for holy is "qodesh" which means "apartness, sacredness," or "separateness" showing that God is altogether holy, sacred, set apart, or separate from His creation.

As believers, we can understand God's attributes such as love, mercy, and grace, but holiness is an attribute of God that is not shared with humans. Although a person who repents and trusts in Christ has Jesus' own righteousness accredited to their account, that is not the same as having inherent holiness.

> 2 Corinthians 5:21 "He made Him who knew no sin to be sin in our behalf, so that we might become the righteousness of God in Him."

In fact, God is so holy that no one on earth could look at Him and live (Ex 33:20). It would be like looking at the sun and going blind as a result, but God's holiness and being in His presence would do more than that.

Our holiness as believers is our being separated from this world and united to God in His Holiness.

> 1 Peter 1:14-16 "As obedient children, do not be conformed to the former lusts which were yours in your ignorance, 15but like the Holy One who called you, be holy yourselves also in all your behavior; 16because it is written: "You shall be holy for I am Holy."

What does it mean that God is holy? Holiness is absolute perfection. God is unlike any other and His holiness is the essence of that "otherness." His very being is completely absent of even a trace of sin. He is high above any other, and no one can compare to Him. God's holiness saturates His entire being and shapes all His attributes. His love is a holy love, His mercy is holy mercy, and even His anger and wrath are holy anger and holy wrath. These concepts are difficult for humans to grasp, just as God is difficult for us to understand in His entirety.

Day and night these angels did not fail to worship God, who is worthy of glory honor, and praise.

As John watched in amazement, the living creatures gave glory, honor, and thanks to Him who sits on the throne, to Him who lives forever and ever.

John continued to watch intently at the worship. The twenty-four elders will fall down before Him who sits on the throne, and they will worship Him who lives forever and ever, and will cast their crowns before the throne, saying, "Worthy are You, our Lord and our God, to receive glory and honor and power; for You created all things, and because of Your will they existed and were created."

The twenty-four elders cast down their crowns before the Lord as a way to worship God. By doing this they were saying to God, I do not deserve this God. I am not worthy of anything that you have to offer. I am not even worthy to be in your presence. It is only because of Jesus Christ, who died for our sins and gives us salvation. This is why the body of believers will lay their crowns before God, because we are not worthy.

Who was deserving of the majesty, the honor, and the praise? None but God! In their worship, they indicated that despite what they may have done on earth to earn these crowns, only God is truly worthy of glory and honor.

In the presence of the Lord Jesus Himself, all good deeds we have done will pale in comparison. How do we get to heaven in the first place? Only through Jesus Christ who died for our sins, paying the atonement for the penalty for us. We have done nothing to earn heaven or eternity. We have been saved through the grace and mercy of God and God alone.

> Ephesians 2:8-9 "For by grace you have been saved through faith; and this is not of yourselves, it is the gift of God; 9 not a result of works, so that no one may boast."

The crown of life we are given by God is due to His working, His salvation, His grace and mercy, and for His majesty. For those who trust in Christ, we are all sinners who have been forgiven by Jesus' death upon the cross.

What can we boast about in our life? Nothing. We are all sinners. Even when we accept Christ as our Savior we continue to fall into our selfish desires to please ourselves before God. The forgiveness that Christ offers us overcomes all of our sins.

The truth is, Jesus has paid for the sins of the entire world. "He is the atoning sacrifice for our sins, and not only for ours, but also for the sins of the whole world" (I John 2:2). If sin were atoned for, then by Jesus' blood we are forgiven by God. But yet, what can we boast about? We can only boast about our precious Savior and the love of God. This is why the elders laid their crowns down before God. They understood it was only because of God, His sacrifice, and His mercy that they were able to be in His presence.

Even while we are on earth, what can we give to God as a sacrifice of praise? Our very life. Not because we have to, but because we love Him.

> Romans 12:1 "Therefore I urge you, brothers and sisters, by the mercies of God, to present your bodies as a living and holy sacrifice, acceptable to God, which is your spiritual service of worship."

Our worship is not just the songs we sing out of adoration to God, but we should be worshipping the King with our very life.

Yes, we may have not received our crowns of life yet, but right now, we have our life to honor God. To honor God, means to honor Him with the only thing we consider precious to us, our lives.

If I were to ask you who is worthy of one thousand dollars? I am sure some people would say that they are worthy, but why? What makes you worthy of the money? Do you deserve it? Ask the same question of your salvation. What makes you worthy of Jesus' death and sacrifice for your salvation? Nothing. The answer is nothing.

> Romans 3:23-25 "for all have sinned and fall short of the glory of God, 24 being justified as a gift by His grace through the redemption which is in Christ Jesus, 25 whom God displayed publicly as a propitiation in His blood through faith. This was to demonstrate His

righteousness, because in God's merciful restraint He let the sins previously committed go unpunished;"

What do we deserve? Eternity in hell. We deserve eternal separation from God and the eternal punishment for our sins. Even the best we can do on this earth is considered as filthy rags.

Isaiah 64:6 "For all of us have become like one who is unclean, And all our righteous deeds are like a filthy garment; And all of us wither like a leaf, And our wrongdoings, like the wind, take us away."

If you were to think about how good we are, let us estimate how many times a person sins in a day? Let's just say the average person sins 20 times a day. Now multiply those sins times seven days a week. That would be 140 sins a week. Now take the 140 sins and multiply those times fifty-two weeks a year.

That brings our total sins in a year to 7,280. If we were to estimate that our life span on this earth would be the age of 85 years of age and we multiply our sins for each year, this would bring us to a total of 618,800 sins in a lifetime. Just one sin is too much before a holy God.

How many sins can Jesus forgive? All but one, the sin of rejecting Him as your Savior. Jesus will never force you to accept His free gift of salvation. He only offers it to us.

None of us are worthy. The crowns of life are not by our works, but Christ in us. God gives us heaven, He gives us eternity, He gives us the privilege to be joint-heirs with Jesus, and He gives us everything that we do not deserve.

> Revelation 4:11 "Worthy are You, our Lord and our God, to receive glory and honor and power; for You created all things, and because of Your will they existed, and were created."

5

WHO IS WORTHY?

IN ARTHURIAN LEGENDS, EXCALIBUR WAS KING ARTHUR'S MAGIC SWORD. It was said that the Lady of the Lake had entrusted a magical sword, Excalibur, to the magician Merlin. Merlin, knowing the power of the sword, knew that it should only be wielded by the true King of England. To keep anyone who was truly unworthy from wielding the sword of power, Merlin plunged the sword into a solid boulder on the outskirts of the land. He said, "Whoever pulled the sword from the stone would be the next king of England." Though many tried to pull the sword from the stone, it remained firmly fixed there. Some of the strongest men in the land attempted to pull the sword out, but none succeeded until the young Arthur pulled it out with ease.

> Revelation 5:1-5 "I saw in the right hand of Him who sat on the throne a scroll written inside and on the back, sealed up with seven seals. 2 And I saw a strong angel proclaiming with a loud voice, "Who is worthy to open the scroll and to break its seals?" 3 And no one in heaven or on the earth or under the earth was able to open the scroll or to look into it. 4 Then I began to weep greatly because no one was found worthy to open the scroll or to look into it.

5 And one of the elders *said to me, "Stop weeping; behold, the Lion that is from the tribe of Judah, the Root of David, has overcome so as to be able to open the scroll and its seven seals."

You may ask why was Jesus the only one who could open the scroll? Because Jesus is the only one who will judge mankind. Jesus came into the world to save those who put their trust in Him, but His coming also brought judgment.

John 5:22-23 "For not even the Father judges anyone, but He has given all judgment to the Son, 23 so that all will honor the Son just as they honor the Father. The one who does not honor the Son does not honor the Father who sent Him."

As all the angels fasten their gaze upon the throne of God. An angel proclaimed, "Who is worthy?" How hard would it be to answer this question, "Who is worthy?" How would John be able to answer this question posed by the angel? John knew he was not worthy, for he was a sinful man. The angels knew that they could never be worthy, for they were just messengers and servants of the Almighty God.

John continued to look around with anticipation, but no one came forward. Sadness invaded John's heart. It overwhelmed his soul. For was there none worthy to open this scroll? John's heart broke as he burst into tears. As John cried tears of sorrow, one of the elders who sat around the throne of God approached John and comforted him by saying, "Stop weeping; behold, the Lion that is from the tribe of Judah, the Root of David, has overcome so as to be able to open the scroll and its seven seals." It is none other than Jesus. John's heart leaped with joy; it was Jesus. He is worthy!

No greater worship exists beyond this statement, "You are worthy Jesus." You alone are worthy. Take that in for a moment. Jesus, who is God, owns it all. He made it all. He reflects the complete radiance of God's glory. He is the exact representation of God's being. He continues to sustain all things and He paid the price for our sin. He rules it all.

The word for both worthy and worship is from the same root word, worth. As we finished reading at the end of Revelation 4:11 "Worthy are You, our Lord and our God, to receive glory and honor and power; for You created all things, and because of Your will they existed, and were created."

We worship that which we believe is of great worth or value. Take for instance gold or money. People worship it because it is of great value to them. There is a great difference between God's value and the value that we assign to the people and the things in life. Take for example your house. If you own a home, your house has a value that is set by the market or by the consumers. You may feel that your house is worth more money than someone is willing to pay. The consumer market determines the value of your home.

The difference between God's worth and the worth of your house is that God's worth does not depend on the market or people. It does not matter how many people recognize or do not recognize His worth; His value remains priceless. God is worthy of glory, honor, and power. He has created everything. Everything of value and everything we value, God made it. He designed it. He molded it. He grew it. He shaped it. He trained it. He provided for it. He inspired it. He prepared it. He helped it. He healed it. He gave it life. God is worthy of worship, and no external circumstances ever change that fact.

> Colossians 1:15-20 "He is the image of the invisible God, the firstborn of all creation: 16 for by Him all things were created, both in the heavens and on earth, visible and invisible, whether thrones, or dominions, or rulers, or authorities all things have been created through Him and for Him. 17 He is before all things, and in Him all things hold together. 18 He is also the head of the body, the church; and He is the beginning, the firstborn from the dead, so that He Himself will come to have first place in everything. 19For it was the Father's good pleasure for all the fullness to dwell in Him, 20and through Him to reconcile all things to Himself, whether things on earth or things in heaven, having made peace through the blood of His cross."

> Psalm 145:3 "Great is the LORD, and highly to be praised; And His greatness is unsearchable."

The more we get to know God, the more we want to worship Him. When we worship God, we are praising God and proclaiming His worthiness of our time, our attention, our adoration, our praise, and our love. Worship is not just music, though the music is an outpouring of our worship. It's not the melody, the rhythm, or the lyrics. Worship is not whether we lift our hands or we clap our hands when we praise Him.

All of these things are expressions of worship. The worship we give springs from the love that we have for God. The inner essence of worship is the response of the heart to the knowledge of the mind. When the mind is rightly understanding God then the heart is rightly valuing God.

Here is the key to the heart of worship, we can only worship someone we love and we can only love someone we know. When people look at a Christian's life, they should be able to tell how much God really means to them. They should see His value. They should be able to tell God's value in our lives by how much we invest in our relationship with God. A Christian's life should properly reflect how much God is worth to them. The word that God uses for "know" describes more than the desire to have knowledge about Him, it implies intimacy. God calls us to pursue an intimate and experiential knowledge of Him and it is in that knowledge of Him that brings forth our true worship.

I can see John saying to himself over and over again in his mind, "Jesus is worthy, Jesus is worthy" until these thoughts want to leap from his chest and cheer with a loud voice, "Jesus is worthy!" John watched with anticipation as Jesus stood at the throne. The lamb who was slain for us.

At that moment, Jesus took the scroll from the Father's hand and tightened His grip upon it. The believers who surrounded the throne fell before Him, He who was worthy.

Revelation 5:6-8 "And I saw between the throne (with the four living creatures) and the elders a Lamb standing, as if slaughtered, having seven horns and seven eyes, which are the seven spirits of God sent out into all the earth. 7 And He came and took the scroll out of the right hand of Him who sat on the throne. 8 When He had taken the scroll, the four living creatures and the twenty-four elders fell down before the Lamb, each one holding a harp and golden bowls full of incense, which are the prayers of the saints."

John could not help but bow in reverence to Jesus. He laid down upon the ground. His face laid on the golden sea of glass as he must have thought, "Jesus you are worthy." Then off in the distance sweet melodies of music began to play. It was a song for the redeemer. The songs began to lift up one by one as all voice's of heaven began to sing in unison, "Worthy are You to take the scroll and to break its seals; for You were slaughtered, and You purchased people for God with Your blood from every tribe, language, people, and nation. You have made them into a kingdom and priests to our God, and they will reign upon the earth." (Revelation 5:9)

We are not worthy of anything Jesus has to offer. Because of our salvation purchased by His blood, our lives should be constant praise to His name, for He alone is worthy. He is worthy of praise because of who He is, what He has done, and what He continued to do.

6

THE IMPERSONATOR
AND THE HORSEMEN

As John watched with anticipation of the scroll that Jesus held in His hand, little did John know what was about to happen. After the rapture of the church occurs, this world will enter the beginning of the Tribulation Period

The Tribulation Period is what the future holds, as a seven-year period of time, when God will finish His discipline of those on earth while also trying to redeem the Jewish people and finalize His judgment of the unbelieving world. The tribulation will be a terrible time, but it will serve a purpose. It will warn mankind of God's imminent judgment.

THE FIRST SEAL

> Revelation 6:1-2 "Then I saw when the Lamb broke one of the seven seals, and I heard one of the four living creatures saying as with a voice of thunder, "Come!" 2 I looked, and behold, a white horse, and the one who sat on it had a bow; and a crown was given to him, and he went out conquering and to conquer."

Just after the rapture, there will exist a state of confusion on earth. Remember that all believers have been removed from this earth causing mass confusion and hysteria. It will seem like the end of the world for most people. How do you explain roughly two billion people missing from all over the earth? Those who are left behind will be distraught, looking for answers to where all these people have gone. In this mass confusion enters a person who will promise peace, safety, and solace for the confusion. It will be during this moment that the Anti-Christ comes into play.

As John sees the first seal break, a loud crack of thunder roared across heaven. As John looked upon the earth a strong and brazen figure appeared from the sea of men. He was bold and dynamic, well-spoken, and well-groomed. His deminer showed the confidence of a leader. His elegant style charmed the hearts of the people who were quickly drawn to him.

John sees a symbol of a man on a white horse who carried a bow. This man's mission was for the purpose of peacefully conquering the people. This person comes as a messiah and a savior for all those who have been left behind. This savior of the people is very different than Jesus. Jesus came to save, but this man comes to conquer.

When we read the name Antichrist, the prefix anti can also mean "instead of," and both meanings will apply to this coming world leader. He will overtly oppose Christ and at the same time pass himself off as Christ.

Take notice and compare for a moment that at the end of the book of Revelation, when Jesus comes back to fight the final Battle of Armageddon, and the way the first rider comes in Revelation 6.

> Revelation 6:2 "I looked, and behold, a white horse, and the one who sat on it had a bow; and a crown was given to him, and he went out conquering and to conquer."
>
> Revelation 19:11-12 "And I saw heaven opened, and behold, a white horse, and He who sat on it is called Faithful and True, and in righteousness He judges and wages war. 12 His eyes are a flame of fire, and on His head are many crowns; and He has a name written on Him which no one knows except Himself."

Do you see the difference? When Rome's generals would return from war victorious, they would parade down the main street on a white horse.

The bow speaks of military might, and the crown is a champion's crown. When a Roman general, had been victorious in battle, he returned home to celebrate his victory. He then paraded up and down the streets to receive the praise of the people.

At the beginning of the tribulation, it is the Antichrist who tries to be the impersonator of the Savior.

How will he bring peace? Through conquering. The Bible is clear that one man, the Antichrist, will rise up to unite the world under one government during the tribulation. This global dictator will pose as an angel of light, just like his father the devil, but will later act out of his true, evil nature as he proclaims himself as god.

How will he be able to bring peace? It is my belief that he will bring all people together to face a single enemy. How will this impersonator give understanding to what has just occurred on earth? He will not give the truth. It is my belief that he will say our world has been attacked by aliens. I know it sounds strange, but how else would you describe all the missing people of this world, without giving the truth of what really happened? Even in our society today how many movies do we have of alien abductions? How else will people explain the disappearance?

The Antichrist will try to focus people on one enemy, the one who took all the missing people. If you remember the day on September 2001, when the planes had been highjacked and flown into the World Trade Centers, the United States came together to face a single enemy. It was just after that day that in our country more American flags had been sold than any other day. Why? Because we were coming together as a nation to face our enemy.

The Antichrist will promise peace and promise to provide for all those who are still here on earth. He will take dominion over every government and power and bring them all under himself as the leader of this world. During this time the world will be ruled by the fittest for survival. There will be times of looting, stealing, and robbing.

As John looked, he saw another symbol of the rider on a red horse. This horse was not one of peace, but of war.

THE SECOND SEAL

> Revelation 6:3-4 "When He broke the second seal, I
> heard the second living creature saying, "Come!" 4 And
> another, a red horse, went out; and to him who sat on
> it, it was granted to take peace from the earth, and that
> people would kill one another; and a large sword was
> given to him."

The rider on the red horse responds to the command to come
and receives permission to take peace from the earth. Apparently, a
measure of international peace will prevail at the beginning of the
tribulation. Paul warned in 1 Thessalonians 5:3 that "while people are
saying, 'There is peace and security,' then sudden destruction will come
upon them." This war that will take place will not only be between
countries trying to seize power in the unrest of the world, but it will be
state against state, neighborhood versus neighborhoods. It will be war
throughout the whole world as people fight for survival and supplies.
Anarchy will be running rampant throughout the streets as wars will
overtake and destroy many people's lives.

Throughout the history of the world, there has only been about
eight percent of history that has been a time of peace. Look at the time
of war through our history.

- In 1775 during the Revolutionary War, 36,863 were killed.
- 1792 Napoleonic War -1,079,574
- 1861 Civil War -2,456,000
- 1898 Spanish War- 6,457

- 1889 Philippine War- 24,064

- 1937 World War I- 13,770,201

- 1941 World War II- 26,500,000

In my lifetime, the United States military has fought in Lebanon 1982-1983, Grenada 1983, Panama 1989-1990, the Persian Gulf War 1990, Iraq 2001, and Afghanistan 2009-2020.

Even just recently Russia has just attacked Ukraine in an act of war. It is common to hear of wars still continuing throughout our day and time, but nothing so much as will be seen when the red horseman is unleashed.

The stages are set for the events of the Tribulation described in the Bible. The White Horse and the Red Horse are just on the horizon, like never before in earth's history. Not only will there be worldwide conquest and worldwide conflict, but a terrible plague is yet to come. The minds of the people will be on surviving, as people will be in fear for their lives. Peace will not be on people's minds survival will be.

John gasped as he watched the destruction caused by the red horseman. The evil in men's minds and hearts, the lust for power and destruction made John sick to his stomach. So many lives were lost as he watched the atrocities of the world. What could he say? How could he stand to watch all this death? Just then the sound of another seal that was being broken by Jesus. John spun to look upon Jesus and then turned back to look as another devastating horseman made his way onto the earth.

THE THIRD SEAL

> Revelation 6:5-6 "When He broke the third seal,
> I heard the third living creature saying, "Come!" I
> looked, and behold, a black horse, and the one who
> sat on it had a pair of scales in his hand. 6 And I heard
> something like a voice in the center of the four living
> creatures saying, "A quart of wheat for a denarius, and
> three quarts of barley for a denarius; and do not damage
> the oil and the wine."

The third Horseman rode a black horse. It was the horseman that
would bring famine upon the earth.

John watched as it seemed as if the earth was drying up. The fields
were becoming desolate. The food was becoming scarce. But why did
this horseman have a pair of scales?

In this symbol, the horseman carried a pair of balances or weighing
scales, indicating the way that bread would have been weighed during a
famine. In the Bible, wheat was measured and not weighed. Balances are
used to weigh precious things, but here a balance is used for measuring
wheat.

With all the destruction from the bombs and missiles sent from
other countries, and with the destruction occurring from the farmer's
fields as battles take place around our own homes, it seems as if the
plentiful harvest that we now enjoy in our world, will be gone.

The passage indicates the price of grain is about ten times the
normal price. An entire day's wages, a denarius, would only give you

enough wheat for only one person. Workers would struggle to have enough to feed their families, let alone themself. During this time people will be starving, barely able to meet their basic needs.

During the time of famine, even oil and wine cannot be wasted. In the past two thousand years, wars, famine, earthquakes, and so forth have occurred more frequently as time draws nearer. The balances reveal scarcity. Americans do not worry about the availability of food in times of plenty. In these future days, the price of food will skyrocket while millions have no access to any food. Worldwide famine is not hard to imagine. We can witness it now in Central and Eastern Africa.

In a survey done of the world population, it is estimated that eleven people are likely dying every minute from hunger, now outpacing COVID-19 fatalities. At least 155 million people around the world are now living in crisis levels of food insecurity, and more than 520,000 people are on the brink of starvation. (Oxfam International Published: 9th July 2021)

If this is happening in our world now, what will it be like when people go through the tribulation?

THE FORTH SEAL

> Revelation 6:7-8 "When the Lamb broke the fourth seal, I heard the voice of the fourth living creature saying, "Come!" 8 I looked, and behold, an ashen horse; and the one who sat on it had the name Death, and Hades was following with him.

Authority was given to them over a fourth of the earth,

to kill with sword, and famine, and plague, and by the

wild animals of the earth."

The word "ashen" is the same as the word "green" found in Mark 6:39, Revelation 8:7, and 9:4. A green complexion indicates either sickness or death. This is why the name of the one riding on the pale horse is "Death." The word "death" in the second part of the verse can be translated as "pestilence." Therefore, we interpret it as "pestilence" here also.

"Hades" in the original language means the unseen world. Hades here is like a trash can because so many people are dying.

The people will become so desensitized to death that collecting the bodies is as common as collecting trash. Millions of people all over the world will die.

As we are told in verse 8; over a fourth of the earth, are killed by the sword of the red horse, by the famine of the black horse, by the death of the pale horse, and by the beasts."

The current population of the world is nearly 7.6 billion people. If we take out the estimated believers of the world, it would be most likely 5 billion people who would be on the earth during the tribulation. That means more than 1.25 billion people would die in this first wave of trouble during the tribulation. They would die as a result of war, famine, disease, and wild animals.

In March 1918, there was the Spanish Flu, in 2014 the world was worried about Ebola. In 2020, the world found itself plagued with

Covid-19. There's no question, the stage is set for worldwide plagues to devastate the planet just as it is predicted here in Revelation 6.

Not only war, famine, plague, but wild animals. Yes, wild animals. Not only will man fear his next-door neighbor, but he will also have to be cautious of the animals looking to survive.

Some animal predators exhibit a pattern of hunting humans akin to that of a serial killer. It's been well documented all around the world that when a wild animal kills a human, it often goes on a rampage not just ending with one human life, but many. The biggest issue is that once a predator has started to identify humans as food, they may begin actively seeking to hunt and feed off more humans. It is not because we are delicious, it is the fact we are comparatively plentiful and at least appear to be relatively safe to hunt.

This is why the United States National Parks Service has protocols to kill bears that maul or stalk humans after tasting their flesh.

The risk of predatory events will skyrocket once an animal starts thinking of humans as relatively harmless, and more as plentiful piles of walking meals. Once they have a taste of human blood though, they stop seeing us as these dangerous creatures, but more so as a potential source of food.

Everything will be in place for worldwide conquest, worldwide conflict, worldwide hunger, and worldwide death. The Bible teaches that the world is headed not toward peace and unity, but toward a final, cataclysmic war, the Battle of Armageddon. Things on this earth will continue to deteriorate as the world falls deeper and deeper into chaos, confusion, and sin.

As we have seen the first four seals clearly describe frightening judgments without parallel in human history. There is nothing that has yet happened since John had this vision that could be the fulfillment of these judgments.

John looked distraught at the things he had seen with his own eyes. So many people were killed and died from the devastation of these horsemen. So much destruction. What has the world come to? The evil of men, with no thought to the killing and murder of so many people. John stood there silent with his hand over his mouth. "So many", he thought. "Billions of people, are now dead and suffering in hell." This thought was too overwhelming for John.

What has he just seen? At that moment, the sound of another seal had been broken.

THE FIFTH SEAL

> Revelation 6:9-11 "When the Lamb broke the fifth seal, I saw underneath the altar the souls of those who had been killed because of the word of God, and because of the testimony which they had maintained; 10 and they cried out with a loud voice, saying, "How long, O Lord, holy and true, will You refrain from judging and avenging our blood on those who live on the earth?"

11 And a white robe was given to each of them; and they were told that they were to rest for a little while longer, until the number of their fellow servants and their brothers and sisters who were to be killed even as they had been, was completed also."

As John sees the fifth seal open, it did not deal with judgment, as the other seals before had, but it dealt with the ones who were saved during the tribulation period. During the tribulation, believers are not here to conquer the earth. We are not here to rule. We are supposed to be holding on to the testimony of Jesus Christ. During this time, God has allowed the Antichrist to take power and to take peace from the earth. When Jesus breaks the fifth seal, John sees, under the altar the souls of those who had been slain for the word of God and for the testimony which they held.

Shortly after the beginning of the tribulation, there will be a great "soul harvest" in the world. After the people see what happened in the rapture, millions will come to faith in Jesus. Christians will be martyred for their belief as the Antichrist takes power.

What did you expect with the Antichrist? Did you expect him to leave the believers alone? Did you think Christianity would be a life of ease? Did you think it would be a walk in the park?

Throughout the book of Revelation, we find that the imagery intensifies. I saw under the altar the souls of those who had been slain. Not only are these the souls of those who have died, but these are also the souls of those who have been killed.

These are the souls of those who have died a violent death. These are the souls of those who have been stoned, who have been beheaded, who have been hanged, and who have been sawn in two. These are the souls of those who have been counted as sheep for the slaughter. For what reason have they been slain? For the Word of God and for the testimony which they held.

These are the martyrs who have died for their faith, those who have died for the Word of God. They have been killed because they refused to recant Jesus Christ. They have been killed because they held to the Word of God, though it cost them their life.

These believers were martyred because they held fast to the Scriptures. Marshalled under Satan, hostile unbelievers have always aggressively opposed believers. History includes many accounts of evil cultures taking the lives of God's people. Such hatred of believers will reach a boiling point in the tribulation.

"With a loud voice, they cried, How long, O Lord, holy and true, will You refrain from judging and avenging our blood on those who live on the earth?"

This is just the beginning of the tribulation period. God did not give us a timeline of exactly how far apart the events take place throughout the book of Revelation. As of this point, it could have been three months from the seals being broken or one year. With all that has taken place on the earth, what we have seen so far will be nothing in comparison to what comes next.

As John listened intently to their cries, he looked upon those who had died for their belief in Christ, he understood the need for the Lord to avenge all the believers who had been persecuted for their trust in God.

But John pondered the one-word God had given to the martyrs, "Rest". Rest in God's timeline. Rest in God's power. Rest in God's sovereignty.

At this time, it seems that believers in heaven are aware of God's activity with respect to judging unrighteousness and establishing righteousness on the earth. In fact, they are passionately concerned about seeing righteousness prevail! They do not have a passive disinterest in what happens on earth; but they share God's passion for seeing His enemies judged, sin and Satan defeated, the fallen earth restored, and Christ exalted overall.

John thought intently at the word "rest." How could he rest in what he had seen so far? The evil of men, the prevailing of the Antichrist, and the death to those who believed in the one true God, Yahweh.

Before John could even finish his thought, another seal was broken, and John's eyes looked down at the sight of the next seal.

THE SIXTH SEAL

> Revelation 6:12-17 "And I looked when He broke the sixth seal, and there was a great earthquake; and the sun became as black as sackcloth made of hair, and the whole moon became like blood; 13 and the stars of the sky fell to the earth, as a fig tree drops its unripe figs when shaken by a great wind. 14 The sky was

split apart like a scroll when it is rolled up, and every mountain and island was removed from its place.

15 Then the kings of the earth and the eminent people, and the commanders and the wealthy and the strong, and every slave and free person hid themselves in the caves and among the rocks of the mountains;"

16 "and they said to the mountains and the rocks, "Fall on us and hide us from the sight of Him who sits on the throne, and from the wrath of the Lamb; 17 for the great day of Their wrath has come, and who is able to stand?"

What was happening to the universe? John watched as a great earthquake shook the world. The whole earth seemed to tremble as if someone had grabbed hold of the earth and violently shook it as to move the earth from its foundations.

The sun stopped emitting the rays of light as a dim blackness filled its globe, saturating the light with darkness. As the sun's light diminished, the glow of the moon turned to a deep red, as if blood had been poured over its surface, and it gave an eerie incandescent glow. John watched as the stars had started falling from the sky landing with an eruption of blows upon the earth one after another, each one striking the earth with a loud crashing sound as they hit the earth. The sky grew black and the cloud rolled back as if you had taken a piece of paper and rolled it in your hand.

As we try to understand what John is seeing, many people have tried to speculate what is taking place on the earth. Remember what

John is describing is only what he knows from his time. He does not understand the things we see in our society today.

Many explanations have been made about what is happening. Can God do this by his power? Absolutely. But let me pose another possibility to you on what John may be seeing. Not scriptural, but a possibility.

Throughout our earth, we have many active volcanos. If the earth shook with an act of great vengeance, there is a possibility that those dormant and active volcanos, might have their fishers broken open.

The sky would be littered with volcanic ash that plummets hundreds of miles into the sky causing the sky to be blackened and the moon to look red. Even as John sees the sky roll back as a scroll, it could be the very ash as it rises from the volcanos.

Volcanoes are often triggered or accompanied by earthquakes, which are directly mentioned in Bible prophecy. Jesus Christ included earthquakes in His famous Olivet Prophecy. He prophesied, "famines, pestilences, and earthquakes in various places" (Matthew 24:7).

In A.D. 79, Mount Vesuvius erupted and wiped out the Roman cities of Pompeii and Herculaneum. The explosion of the volcano was so sudden, the residents were killed while in their daily routine: men and women were at the market, the rich in their luxurious baths, and slaves at work. They died amid volcanic ash and superheated gasses. It takes little imagination to picture their panic on that terrible day.

Are there in fact volcanoes large enough to cause such an apocalypse? Most people do not know what is referred to as a supervolcano. The term "supervolcano" implies a volcanic center that has had an eruption of magnitude 8 on the Volcano Explosivity Index (VEI), meaning that at one point in time it erupted more than 1,000 cubic kilometers (240 cubic miles) of material. Supervolcanoes can be hidden in oceans or even right below us. There are at least eight supervolcanoes around the world. If every supervolcano went off, you'd have a hard time finding a safe place to flee to, because almost every continent is home to at least one supervolcano.

When a normal volcano erupts, it explodes through the top of the mountain leaving a violent hole in the top of the mountain. When an extremely large eruption occurs, it leaves something called a caldera. A caldera does not look like a regular volcano. It is structured more as a circular-shaped depression in the earth. The calderas have relatively steep walls and are typically tens of miles across.

The caldera forms by rocks settling down into what used to be the magma chamber. There are several super volcanos or calderas within the United States. Yellowstone National Park in Wyoming is one of these large volcanic craters measuring 35 to 45 miles across. If a supervolcano does erupt, the prospects for the world would be devastating.

Let's say you were lucky enough to survive this first wave of destruction from the volcano. After that, it would be hard to find a fallout shelter, because these super-eruptions spew billions of tons of ash, volcanic glass, and rock thousands of meters into the air. It would collapse buildings, contaminate water supplies, and bring down any power grids in its path. And the fallout would extend for hundreds of miles, so any cities nearby a supervolcano would be leveled.

A second possibility is that John may be seeing the after-effects of a nuclear war. Remember that the earth has just gone through a period of time when the whole world was at war. John said, "there was a great earthquake; and the sun became as black as sackcloth made of hair, and the whole moon became like blood; and the stars of the sky fell to the earth, as a fig tree drops its unripe figs when shaken by a great wind. The sky was split apart like a scroll when it is rolled up, and every mountain and island was removed from its place."

Have you ever seen a nuclear bomb detonated? After the impending blast, there would be an immediate destruction of cities, with the potential aftermath of firestorms, a nuclear winter, widespread radiation sickness from fallout, or the temporary, if not a permanent loss of much modern technology due to electromagnetic pulses.

When a nuclear bomb goes off there is a distinct mushroom cloud that rises into the sky looking as if the sky is being rolled back as a scroll.

A Nuclear Winter could be occurring. Nuclear Winter is the term for describing the climatic effects of nuclear war. Smoke from the fires started by nuclear weapons, especially the black soot smoke from cities and industrial facilities would be heated by the sun, rise into the upper stratosphere, and spread globally, lasting for years. The resulting cool, dark, dry conditions at Earth's surface would prevent crop growth for at least one year, resulting in mass starvation over most of the world.

Another reason this is a possibility of what John saw, was that he was using the phrase; "stars of the sky fell to the earth, as a fig tree drops its unripe figs when shaken by a great wind." John has never seen a missile or a bomb heading to its target. In his eyes, these may look like stars falling from the sky, but they may truly be missiles carrying bombs.

Now understand that God does not need man-made events for this to happen. He is God. He could do this without the means of men. But the example that I have just listed for you could be a possibility, we do not know.

What we do know is that whatever causes this event, utter devastation will be throughout the whole world. The kings of this earth will flee in horror to safe places to hide from what is taking place.

Even now our world leaders have created hidden bunkers in the bases of mountains to hide from such an event. In the United States, we have Norad base command in Cheyenne Mountain in Colorado, Russia has Yamantau Mountain. In China, there is Wunjian Mountain near Dazhi. Many leaders throughout the world have prepared for such an event as nuclear war or the apocalypse, but no matter how people prepare, no one can hide from God's judgment.

I can imagine John wanting to plead for those on earth, but who is he to say anything about what is occurring.

God has given every person a chance to have the gift of salvation, but those who are left behind either rejected God's gift or denied His existence.

This picture reveals that judgment is in the hands of God, not Satan. God is a just judge, He's gracious and merciful, but always just. God's judgments have our redemption as their goal.

7

THE SEAL OF GOD

REVELATION 7:1–8 "AFTER THIS I SAW FOUR ANGELS standing at the four corners of the earth, holding back the four winds of the earth so that no wind would blow on the earth, or on the sea, or on any tree. 2 And I saw another angel ascending from the rising of the sun, holding the seal of the living God; and he called out with a loud voice to the four angels to whom it was granted to harm the earth and the sea, 3 saying, "Do not harm the earth, or the sea, or the trees until we have sealed the bond-servants of our God on their foreheads. 4 And I heard the number of those who were sealed: 144,000, sealed from every tribe of the sons of Israel: 5 from the tribe of Judah, twelve thousand were sealed, from the tribe of Reuben twelve thousand, from the tribe of Gad twelve thousand, 6 from the tribe of Asher twelve thousand, from the tribe of Naphtali twelve thousand, from the tribe of Manasseh twelve thousand, 7 from the tribe of Simeon twelve thousand, from the tribe of Levi twelve thousand, from the tribe of Issachar twelve thousand, 8 from the tribe of Zebulun twelve thousand, from the tribe of Joseph twelve thousand,

and from the tribe of Benjamin, twelve thousand were sealed."

As John watched, the earth became still. Four angels posed themselves at the four corners of the earth. The gentle winds that roamed the earth suddenly stopped blowing. He saw an angel come from over the horizon to announce the destruction must halt for a brief moment. In this momentary pause, the angel lifted his voice to announce those who have been chosen by God. These 144,000 are believed to be God's evangelists to this world. They all will have the challenge of bringing the good news of the gospel message to the Jewish people.

As John watched, the angel took a seal and placed it upon their foreheads. What was the seal? As he looked in wonder, he finally caught a glimpse of the seal. It's the name of God. It is God's name that had been placed on their foreheads. They belong to God.

What is this seal? A seal is a mark of possession, authority, and power. In ancient times when a document was sealed, wax was dripped upon the document and the author or owner's signet ring was pressed into the wax. Whoever read that document knew who wrote it, and whose authority made the decree. Such seals also showed ownership of possessions. God will seal these 144,000 with His very own name, which shows that they are the exclusive property of the Lord God Himself. This seal upon their foreheads was God's mark of possession and protection. These 144,000 Jews will be protected from God's wrath when it is poured out upon the earth.

Even as believers, we have a seal of God.

> Ephesians 1:13-14 "In Him, you also, after listening to the message of truth, the gospel of your salvation having also believed, you were sealed in Him with the Holy Spirit of the promise, 14 who is the first installment of our inheritance, in regard to the redemption of God's own possession, to the praise of His glory."

Through Jesus Christ, you have been restored and you belong to the King. God can and will keep His own. There is one in heaven who is giving you the endorsement.

> John 6:27; "Do not work for the food that perishes, but for the food that lasts for eternal life, which the Son of Man will give you, for on Him the Father, God, has set His seal."

You will stand before God approved and endorsed because of your relationship with Jesus Christ. Nothing else will get you in the door of heaven. Nothing else will get you into God's presence.

For these 144,000, God's seal on these missionaries gives them safe passage to His people to declare His message. It is so safe that all hell cannot overcome it.

To be identified with Christ and be called "servants of our God" is a powerful privilege. It is the assurance of victory. It is a guarantee of protection and provision. It does not mean the enemy will not be foolish enough to attack, he will. But it means you can overcome by the blood of the Lamb.

John's heart beat inside his chest with an exuberance that made him want to leap with joy. God has not given up on them; He is still at work. John watched as the angel counted all of the Jewish believers who were being sent out. Thousands upon thousands were counted. Not just ten thousand who made themselves available to God, but 144,000!

Just then, a song began to fill John's ears. As he spun around to see who was singing the song, he was overwhelmed to see not the angels worshipping, but a multitude of people, standing behind him, clothed in white robes, waving palm branches. They were not focused on what was happening on earth, they were worshipping Jesus. The song continued to get louder and louder as he heard them sing, "Salvation belongs to our God who sits on the throne, and to the Lamb." Oh, the song of all these people who worshipped the Lamb. The melody rang throughout John's ears, "Salvation belongs to our God who sits on the throne, and to the Lamb." John found himself joining in song to praise the one who brings life and hope. The praise to the one who has redeemed these people to bring them into a relationship with God.

Tears filled John's eyes as he sang along with them to praise the Lamb who redeemed their lives. Just then the angels join in song, as the people fell down and worshiped Him.

The song became more beautiful than before as the voices resounded the song of, "Amen, blessing, glory, wisdom, thanksgiving, honor, power, and might belong to our God forever and ever. Amen."

Revelation 7:9-12 "After these things I looked, and behold, a great multitude which no one could count, from every nation and all the tribes, peoples, and languages, standing before the throne and before the Lamb, clothed in white robes, and palm branches were in their hands; 10 and they cried out with a loud voice, saying, "Salvation belongs to our God who sits on the throne, and to the Lamb." 11 And all the angels were standing around the throne and around the elders and the four living creatures; and they fell on their faces before the throne and worshiped God, 12 saying "Amen, blessing, glory, wisdom, thanksgiving, honor, power, and might belong to our God forever and ever. Amen."

So caught in worship, John had stopped writing what he was seeing and praised God right along with those who worshipped before the King. As John worshipped with praise, one of the elders came to John and asked, do you know who these people are? "These are the ones who come out of the great tribulation, and they have washed their robes and made them white in the blood of the Lamb. For this reason, they are before the throne of God, and they serve Him day and night in His temple; and He who sits on the throne will spread His tabernacle over them. They will no longer hunger nor thirst, nor will the sun beat down on them, nor any scorching heat; for the Lamb in the center of the throne will be their shepherd, and will guide them to springs of the water of life, and God will wipe every tear from their eyes."

Revelation 7:13-17 "Then one of the elders responded, saying to me, "These who are clothed in the white robes, who are they, and where have they come from?" 14 I said to him, "My lord, you know." And he said to me, "These are the ones who come out of the great tribulation, and they have washed their robes and made them white in the blood of the Lamb. 15 For this reason they are before the throne of God, and they serve Him day and night in His temple; and He who sits on the throne will spread His tabernacle over them. 16 They will no longer hunger nor thirst, nor will the sun beat down on them, nor any scorching heat; 17 for the Lamb in the center of the throne will be their shepherd, and will guide them to springs of the water of life; and God will wipe every tear from their eyes."

John was amazed. So many people were saved from the tribulation. So many lives were touched because of Christ. At that moment, of seeing all of those who had trusted Christ, John turned again to Jesus and began singing as if he had never stopped, praising and glorifying Jesus. He never wanted the praise to stop. In that next moment, Jesus held up the scroll in His hand to break the last seal.

8

THE TRUMPETS OF JUDGEMENT

AT THAT MOMENT WITH THE BREAKING OF THE SEVENTH SEAL, everything stopped. Nothing but silence.

THE SEVENTH SEAL

Revelation 8:1 "When the Lamb broke the seventh seal, there was silence in heaven for about half an hour."

Never since the time of creation, has there ever been silence in heaven. There was no worship, no songs of praise, no instruments, nothing. Just the deafening sound of silence. Why is there silence?

What could stop the glory and praise of God? In that moment of silence, it seemed as if an eternity had passed. Not a whisper, not a sound. In that silence, seven angels made their way before the throne of God and stood there as if they were waiting for the next command.

> Revelation 8:3-5 "Another angel came and stood at the altar, holding a golden censer; and much incense was given to him, so that he might add it to the prayers of all the saints on the golden altar which was before the throne.

4 And the smoke of the incense ascended from the angel's hand with the prayers of the saints before God. 5 Then the angel took the censer and filled it with the fire of the altar, and hurled it to the earth; and there were peals of thunder and sounds, and flashes of lightning and an earthquake."

John saw an Angel come before the throne of God. In his hand, he held a golden bowl. John continued to observe the angel, and from the bowl rose the smoke of the incense that ascended from the angel's hand, filled with the prayers of the saints before God.

Then in a split moment, the angel took the bowl and flung the incense from the prayers of the saints down upon the earth.

John quickly turned to see as the incense and the prayers of the saint rained down upon the earth, with the sounds of thunder and flashes of lightning. The incense fell upon the earth and a great earthquake shook the earth.

What was about to happen? Was the Lord going to make a decree? Was there a new song to sing? Just then an angel lifted the trumpet to his mouth.

THE FIRST TRUMPET JUDGEMENT

Revelation 8:7 "The first sounded, and there was hail and fire mixed with blood, and it was hurled to the earth; and a third of the earth was burned up, and a third of the trees were burned up, and all the green grass was burned up."

The first angel blew his trumpet. The sound echoed throughout heaven as if a trumpeter was announcing the sound of a king's arrival. The trumpet blast roared over the earth and suddenly there was hail and fire mixed with blood, and it was hurled to the earth. A third of the earth was burned up, and a third of the trees were burned up, and all the green grass was burned up.

What would be the effects of the trumpet upon the earth? When the first trumpet is sounded, immediately hail and fire mixed with blood fell from the sky at an astonishing rate, slamming upon the earth. The earth and the nations will be in turmoil, perplexed by the raging fires that are caused by the hail.

To help understand the effects of this trumpet, the landmass of the earth is approximately 57,491,000 square miles, which makes up 36,794,240,000 acres of land. That would mean 12,264,747,000 acres will be destroyed by this one event.

The frozen balls of hail mixed with fire would cause a devastating blow to almost all the crops of the world. Forest fires will run rampant, buildings and dwellings will be destroyed. Where at this point could you find safety?

Let your imagination run completely wild. Look up into the sky. Can you envision blazes of fire, streams of blood, and great chunks of ice falling upon the earth? Can you imagine all the trees blazing, burning, and going up in smoke? People will be screaming, running, begging, falling over each other to try and run for cover.

Up to this point, you may still be able to live in your barricaded houses if they were not destroyed in the wars, the looting, and the stealing, as people try to survive. You are not a leader of a country, which will be hiding in the midst of the mountains. The only safe place for you will be in the mountains in a cave, as long as there are no trees and shrubbery to catch on fire around you. Also, remember that animals are still out there trying to eat you as they are also trying to survive.

All the comforts that you once experienced will now be destroyed. Your vehicles will be on fire, your homes burning, and shopping centers and gas stations will be destroyed. How will you eat? Where will you get fresh water? The hail mixed with blood has polluted the streams. The water pumping stations will be destroyed. How will you get the essential items to live as you huddle in a cave with a carved stick as your only measure of defending yourself?

Imagine the impact that this will have on the world. Imagine how this would affect not only the balance of nature, but also the food supply. Fruit trees, lumber, animals, homes, and all green grass are gone. There will be devastation on livestock, farmlands, and fruit fields. It will be like a global scorching of earth.

This first trumpet will have a major impact on the earth and life. God's full wrath was yet to be unleashed. The purpose of this judgment was to warn people to repent.

Allen Robinson

THE SECOND TRUMPET JUDGEMENT

> Revelation 8:8-9 "The second angel sounded, and
> something like a great mountain burning with fire was
> hurled into the sea; and a third of the sea became blood,
> 9 and a third of the creatures which were in the sea and
> had life, died; and a third of the ships were destroyed."

John looked on in horror. What had become of the place he called his home? The whole world seemed to be on fire. Everything seemed to be vanishing in a huge ball of smoke. John swung his head towards the throne as he heard another trumpet sound coming from the angels. With this next trumpet, it looked to him as if someone had taken a great mountain, and thrown it towards the earth. A huge boulder of a mountain, covered in fire, was falling from the universe headed straight towards the earth. The mountain-like rock hit the earth with a thunderous thud, slamming into the earth, making the earth seem to shake on its axis. A huge tidal wave rose from the impact, sweeping over the earth with a reign of terror. To John, it may have looked as if a wave was coming upon the sands of the shoreline, but instead of the shoreline, it was over the whole earth. As the mountain hit, a great wave formed high into the heavens causing massive destruction in its wake. The earth shook, as the wave swept through all lands at hurdling speeds.

The Bible says that when this mountain-like object hits the earth, "a third of the sea became blood, and a third of the creatures which were in the sea and had life, died; and a third of the ships were destroyed."

Imagine the impact of what this mountain covered with fire would do.

When a meteorite hits the planet, the bigger the meteorite the more energy is released. The bigger the meteorite the more damage is likely to occur on the ground due to the environmental effects triggered by the impact. Such effects would be a shock wave, like a nuclear blast wiping out anything in its way, heat radiation, earthquakes, and tsunamis.

When the meteorite hits the earth, the earth would shake violently causing a tremendous earthquake likely to kill at least .17 percent of the total population. In a world with four billion people that are still around on the earth, one million people would die from the impact. If people were not in the impact zone, they would not be obliterated, but then 30 percent of the world population would have fatalities caused by thermal radiation. Basically, it would roast humans to death, or at least result in some pretty horrendous burns. If a human survives the burns from the meteorite, the radiation would most likely lead to poisoning or cancer in the end. The impact would cause dust and smoke to rise into the atmosphere preventing sunlight from reaching our world causing the temperatures to plummet.

Just to give you an idea, if a meteorite the size of an apartment hits Earth, this could possibly destroy a small city. If the meteorite was as big as a 20-story building (200 feet on a side), it could have the amount of energy equal to the largest nuclear bombs made today, about 25 to 50 megatons. This size meteorite would flatten reinforced concrete buildings 5 miles (8 kilometers) from ground zero. It would completely destroy most major cities in the United States. If a meteorite of 600 feet were to strike the mid–Atlantic, it would produce a tidal wave 600 feet high, and the heat from the rock would literally broil the fish. The seismic waves would kill even more, and the tidal wave would sink every ship in the Atlantic.

Needless to say, whatever the impact size, the casualties would be overwhelming for the world, leaving it to waste.

John watched as the people scrambled to take stock of what was left. Towering buildings that once stood as monuments to man's achievements, were now rubble and debris that littered the earth. The encompassing fires that raged from the fiery hail mixed with blood left the forests smoldering as burnt embers littered the ground. The stench of death would fill the air. There would be no comforts of home and safety only the devastation of a world that lay in ruin.

THE THIRD TRUMPET JUDGEMENT

> Revelation 8:10-11 "The third angel sounded, and a
> great star fell from heaven, burning like a torch, and it
> fell on a third of the rivers and on the springs of waters.
> 11 The star is named Wormwood; and a third of the
> waters became wormwood, and many people died from
> the waters because they were made bitter."

John heard the sound of the trumpet as another angel blew his trumpet with a deafening reverberation. He watched another star fall from the universe, exploding over the skies of the earth. Its littered debris scattered down to the earth falling like raindrops. It was as if the clouds had given up their rain in the midst of a summer's day. The great star fell to the earth with its small pieces falling into the rivers, sizzling in the cool waters of the rivers below. Men and women would seek the cool waters to quench their thirst and cleanse themselves from the debris from the fires and destruction, but little did they know that the waters had been poisoned by the falling star. The waters did not satisfy, all the waters did was slowly take their life.

There are 4,617 near-earth asteroids that have so far been cataloged. Some have predictable orbits, while others do flybys. Over 1,000 of them are considered to be larger than a half-mile in diameter. There's a 1/10,000 chance that earth could be struck by them. This comet that falls upon the earth will be called Wormwood.

The English rendering "wormwood" refers to the dark green oil produced by the plant, which was used to kill intestinal worms. Wormwood is a bitter poisonous substance, derived from a root that causes drunkenness and eventually death.

The book of Revelation refers to the water being turned into wormwood, making the water undrinkable. When wormwood is digested, it can cause seizures, muscle breakdown, kidney failure, vomiting, stomach cramps, dizziness, tremors, changes in heart rate, urine retention, thirst, numbness of arms and legs, paralysis, and death.

What I find interesting is that in a Ukrainian dictionary, the word "wormwood", is defined as a bitter wild herb used as a tonic. In rural Russia, the word wormwood is translated as Chernobyl. Most of us probably remember the nuclear meltdown at the Chernobyl power plant in 1986, in Russia. When the reactor exploded it sent up a cloud of radiation that spread across Russia, northern Europe, and even reached the shores of North America. Even today 36 years later, the lands around the Chernobyl power plant remain poisoned and still radioactive.

Not only will this trumpet judgment affect one nation, but it will affect the entire world. A third of the world's drinking water will be destroyed.

THE FOURTH TRUMPET JUDGEMENT

> Revelation 8:12-13 "The fourth angel sounded, and a third of the sun, a third of the moon, and a third of the stars were struck, so that a third of them would be darkened and the day would not shine for a third of it, and the night in the same way.13 Then I looked, and I heard an eagle flying in midheaven, saying with a loud voice, "Woe, woe, woe to those who live on the earth, because of the remaining blasts of the trumpet of the three angels who are about to sound!"

John shook his head in disbelief. What was the world coming to? Why would the people not give up their ways and turn to Jesus? Why would people continue to live in evil? Why would they not repent? Because they love themselves more than God. Because they thought of themselves as more important than God.

From the throne, John could hear that another trumpet had sounded. He watched as what occurred next did not affect the earth, but the universe. Something seemed to have impacted the moon, the sun, and the stars of the sky. The sound of the impacts hitting the moon was like a thunderous beating of a bass drum as pieces of the moon began breaking into fragments and littering the sky. The sun, with all its radiance, was somehow hit and now its light was diminished. The bright glow of the sun had now become a dull shimmer of what it once was. The lights around the earth seemed to fade into darkness. The sun which had lighted the days the of earth now only gave two-thirds of its original light, bringing darkness over the face of the earth. Even at night the land became dark for the moon could no longer shine as it once did.

The light we enjoy from the sun and moon have always been considered as God's blessing and a declaration of His glory and faithfulness.

> Psalm 19:1-2 "The heavens tell of the glory of God, And their expanse declares the work of His hands. 2 Day to day pours forth speech, And night to night reveals knowledge."

The fourth angel's trumpet sound struck a third of the sun, moon, and stars. This affected the structure of the universe. Everything from the remaining plant life and even the tides in the oceans would be changed. The natural amount of daylight would be altered. God will supernaturally reduce the intensity of the celestial bodies by one-third. The loss will cause a radical temperature drop, producing severe changes on the earth. The sun and moon's existence are vital to human life, and so lessening their impact upon the earth would send shivers down those who are left.

The judgments from the first three trumpets affected only a third of the land and waters, but this fourth judgment affects the entire world. Why? Because it gets to the very source of the earth's life and energy, the sun. With one-third less sunlight on the earth, there would be one-third less energy available to support the life systems of man and nature. No scientific answer is able to explain adequately these astronomical effects. Apart from the intervention of the sovereign Creator of all things, there can be no explanation. These are the judgments of God going forth in the earth.

At the beginning of Creation, on the fourth day, God brought the sun, moon, and stars into view in order to provide light for man. Under the fourth trumpet, He shall withdraw the light that He Himself created. All of this will affect seriously the health and well-being of people on the earth at that time. During a portion of the day and a portion of the night there will be absolute darkness on the earth.

Not only will nature suffer loss, but human nature will take advantage of the long darkness and no doubt indulge in crime and wickedness.

> John 3:20 "For everyone who does evil hates the Light, and does not come to the Light, so that his deeds will not be exposed."

Now imagine how this will affect mankind. With the loss of one-third of the sun, the days will be cooler, most likely bringing a constant winter to many parts of this world. How many people at this point are prepared with winter clothing and a warm place to stay? How will they stay warm? Remember, due to the hail mixed with fire most of the trees, shrubs, and green grass are gone, so there will be no way to start a fire. People will be huddled in caves trying not to freeze to death, as the days grow short from light.

As the sun goes down, the temperatures drop even more into freezing temperatures. Darkness covers the earth as the moon cannot give the light it once did. Dangers lurk everywhere. Animals looking for you as a meal, and men looking to kill you to take what you have to survive. There you lay huddled in your cave, dying of dehydration from your lack of water, basically slowly dying by starving and freezing to death.

John spoke of an eagle, flying over the earth in the sky, "saying with a loud voice, "Woe, woe, woe to those who live on the earth, because of the remaining blasts of the trumpet of the three angels who are about to sound!" What has happened so far will be nothing compared to what is about to come. How could it get any worse? Although these first four trumpet blasts seemed to be unimaginable, the last three will be off the charts with terror. The first four trumpet judgments were aimed at ecology, the earth, and its environment, but the last three trumpet judgments are directed at man, itself.

Allen Robinson

The Fifth Trumpet Judgement

Revelation 9:1-6 "Then the fifth angel sounded, and I saw a star from heaven which had fallen to the earth; and the key to the shaft of the abyss was given to him. 2 He opened the shaft of the abyss, and smoke ascended out of the shaft like the smoke of a great furnace; and the sun and the air were darkened from the smoke of the shaft. 3 Then out of the smoke came locusts upon the earth, and power was given them, as the scorpions of the earth have power. 4 They were told not to hurt the grass of the earth, nor any green thing, nor any tree, but only the people who do not have the seal of God on their foreheads. 5 And they were not permitted to kill anyone, but to torment for five months; and their torment was like the torment of a scorpion when it stings a person. 6 And in those days, people will seek death and will not find it; they will long to die, and death will flee from them!"

John paced the floor of heaven trying to understand why the men on earth would not turn from their wicked ways and find hope in Jesus? How could they be so blinded? John knew the judgments of God were righteous and just. John knew that God longed for the hearts of men, but men loved themselves more than God.

Notice how John describes what happens. "I saw a star from heaven which had fallen to the earth, and the key to the shaft of the abyss was given to him." How could a star open the pit? Notice the keyword, "him".

Throughout scripture, angels, when mentioned, symbolically, are often described as stars. Many passages in the Bible indeed are talking about angels when they mention stars. Many of these references are found in the Book of Revelation.

> Revelation 12:3-4 "Then another sign appeared in heaven: and behold, a great red dragon having seven heads and ten horns, and on his heads were seven crowns. 4 And his tail swept away a third of the stars of heaven and hurled them to the earth. And the dragon stood before the woman who was about to give birth, so that when she gave birth he might devour her Child."

The reference here describes Satan's fall as he leads one-third of the angels along with him in his rebellion against God.

John was not told when and how the star had fallen, but he was able to tell that the star is an intelligent being to whom acts are ascribed, which could not be said of anything except a living being. As the angel comes from heaven holding the key, he opens the pit, "Then out of the smoke came locusts upon the earth, and power was given them, as the scorpions of the earth have power. They were told not to hurt the grass of the earth, nor any green thing, nor any tree, but only the people who do not have the seal of God on their foreheads."

The supernatural creatures we see released in Revelation 9 are demons or fallen angels. The description given of their appearance is, at the same time, a description of their character. The imagination cannot picture what the earth will be like when it is handed over to the attention of the creatures of hell. These demons, who have been held captive by God in the Bottomless Pit, a place of darkness, smoke, and torment, meant for the evilest angels, are now let loose upon the earth.

The Bottomless Pit was the last place that any fallen angel wanted to be. This bottomless pit was their prison-house. It is an ancient penitentiary for demons, or at least for those demons who are so vile that God keeps them "reserved in chains".

In Luke 8:26-37, Jesus had come upon a man filled with a legion of demons. As Jesus commanded the demons to come out of the man, the demons made one plea to Jesus. They begged not to be sent to the abyss.

> Luke 8:26-37 "Then they sailed to the country of the Gerasenes, which is opposite Galilee. 27 And when He stepped out onto the land, a man from the city met Him who was possessed with demons; and he had not put on clothing for a long time and was not living in a house, but among the tombs. 28 And seeing Jesus, he cried out and fell down before Him, and said with a loud voice, "What business do You have with me, Jesus, Son of the Most High God? I beg You, do not torment me!" 29 For He had already commanded the unclean spirit to come out of the man. For it had seized him many times; and he was bound with chains and shackles and kept under guard, and yet he would break the restraints and be driven by the demon into the desert. 30 And

Jesus asked him, "What is your name?" And he said, "Legion"; because many demons had entered him. 31 And they were begging Him not to command them to go away into the abyss."

The same place the demons begged not to go to was the same place that was now opened by the angel.

2 Peter 2:4 "For if God did not spare angels when they sinned, but cast them into hell and committed them to pits of darkness, held for judgment;"

These demons, who are now released from their imprisonment hate mankind. Their whole purpose is to torture humanity. Notice that even with their power, it is God who controls their terror and limits their power. God has the final say in what happens, not the demons or Satan.

Revelation 9:4-5 "They were told not to hurt the grass of the earth, nor any green thing, nor any tree, but only the people who do not have the seal of God on their foreheads. 5 And they were not permitted to kill anyone, but to torment for five months; and their torment was like the torment of a scorpion when it stings a person."

As John sees these demonic hordes, he describes them as locusts. These are not ordinary locusts. These demons look like locusts, but do not eat the vegetation. They have the power of scorpions in their tails.

These demons are grotesque. Their tails will sting causing horrendous pain with no relief. Their torment of mankind is short-lived, but will still last for five months.

If you have ever been stung by a scorpion you may understand the pain that a scorpion can cause. For those who have never been stung, all scorpion stings cause pain, tingling, and numbness at the sting site. The pain you feel is instantaneous and extreme. The symptoms of a scorpion's sting include: numbness throughout the body, difficulty swallowing, blurred vision, roving eye movements, seizures, salivation, and difficulty breathing. Needless to say, the pain will be like torture. It is not a single sting that men will face, but possibly hundreds or thousands of stings.

Remember these are fallen angels who have the ability to think and to reason. Their whole purpose is to torture. They will do whatever they can to cause pain and suffering to those who do not have the seal of God upon them. There will be no hiding from these demons.

> Revelation 9:7-12 "The appearance of the locusts was like horses prepared for battle; and on their heads appeared to be crowns like gold, and their faces were like human faces. They had hair like the hair of women, and their teeth were like the teeth of lions. They had breastplates like breastplates of iron; and the sound of their wings was like the sound of chariots, of many horses rushing to battle. They have tails like scorpions, and stings; and in their tails is their power to hurt people for five months. They have as king over them, the angel

of the abyss; his name in Hebrew is Abaddon, and in the Greek, he has the name Apollyon."

John sees the angel declare the woes that were yet to come, knowing the first woe has passed and behold, two woes are still coming after these things. How could things get much worse than this? Pain, torture, suffering, dehydration, freezing temperatures, darkness, fear, and hopelessness.

THE SIXTH TRUMPET JUDGEMENT

Revelation 9:13-19 "Then the sixth angel sounded, and I heard a voice from the four horns of the golden altar which is before God, 14 saying to the sixth angel who had the trumpet, "Release the four angels who are bound at the great river Euphrates." 15 And the four angels, who had been prepared for the hour and day and month and year, were released, so that they would kill a third of mankind. 16 The number of the armies of the horsemen was two hundred million; I heard the number of them. 17 And this is how I saw in my vision the horses and those who sat on them: the riders had breastplates the color of fire, of hyacinth, and of brimstone; and the heads of the horses are like the heads of lions; and out of their mouths came fire and smoke and brimstone. 18 A third of mankind was killed

by these three plagues, by the fire, the smoke, and the
brimstone which came out of their mouths."

19 "For the power of the horses is in their mouths and
in their tails; for their tails are like serpents and have
heads, and with them they do harm."

It seemed as if time was one continuous moment, from the sound
of each trumpet followed by the next. Moment by moment, trumpet
by trumpet, each brought forth the destruction of the earth in rapid
succession.

The next trumpet began to blow and the next reign of terror came
upon the earth. John watched as a number of massive troops had formed
right before his eyes. Men and beast whose colors resembled fiery red,
dark blue, and yellow sulfur. The men were mounted for battle, as being
prepared for an invasion. John heard the number of the soldiers. The
count was two hundred million soldiers. How could anyone amass such
a great army? This was more than any army John had ever seen, even in
the Roman Empire. These two hundred million soldiers of evil are very
real and are bent on destruction. John could not believe his own eyes.

The battle had begun. Countless lives of men dying in battle, slain
by the soldier, with piercing noises of explosions and fire. John watched
in disbelief as two hundred million will be bent on killing a third of
mankind was killed by these three plagues, by the fire, the smoke, and
the brimstone which came out of the mouths of the horses.

The tragedies that will befall humankind are far worse than natural
disasters because they are very personal. This chapter records the release
of forces bent on destroying man or inciting him to destroy each other.

To think about beings with that much hate, directed towards mankind is truly frightening.

God's purpose is always redemptive. He wants repentance, not destruction. God will send plagues, war, wild beasts, and earthquakes. God will send natural disasters from space, from volcanoes and He will make the water poisonous and the skies dark.

God will send a demonic plague, the likes of which we have never seen, but despite all of this, men will continue to do evil, living for themselves, which is part of their sinful nature.

The destruction that the sixth trumpet army brings is by fire, smoke, and sulfur. This judgment may be another demonic force.

Another possibility that John may be seeing is an army that uses gunfire and weaponry to fight a battle. John has never seen the effects of guns or gunfire before. Gunpowder was not invented until 904 AD. John died c.100 AD.

To John, it might appear that the horses themselves were belching forth smoke and sulfurous flame, as a mounted army fired weapons against their enemy, bringing death. "The riders had breastplates the color of fire, of hyacinth, and of brimstone; and the heads of the horses are like the heads of lions; and out of their mouths came fire and smoke and brimstone."

It seems that the riders had no offensive weapons, but only the defensive breastplates. They had no active part in carrying out the plague. That was done by the horses. As John describes the description of the horses as nothing he has ever seen on earth. He said, "the heads of the horses resembled the heads of lions." "For the power of the horses is in their mouths and in their tails; for their tails are like serpents and have heads, and with them they do harm."

Now whether this is an army of men sent by the Antichrist, using gunfire to destroy mankind, or an army of demon-like creatures, the end result is still the same, one-third of mankind is killed.

The Bible does not always give us the full details on the destruction, but it brings us to the end results. Look at the results of this destruction so far up to this point.

> Revelation 9:20-21 "The rest of mankind, who were not killed by these plagues, did not repent of the works of their hands so as not to worship demons and the idols of gold, silver, brass, stone, and wood, which can neither see nor hear nor walk; 21 and they did not repent of their murders, nor of their witchcraft, nor of their sexual immorality, nor of their thefts."

Despite all that has occurred on the earth, mankind will not give up its selfish ways. The people did not repent. They continued to worship their idols, they continued in their murders, their drug use, their promiscuity, living for themselves, and refused to worship God.

Now you may have noticed when the word "witchcraft" is used, I used the word "drugs." The word witchcraft comes from the Greek word, pharmakeia (Phar-ma- kee-a), which means, "the use or the administering of drugs, poisoning." This is also where we get our word, "Pharmacy." These people continued to seek out their drugs as the symbol of their worship, refusing to worship God and only doing what we right in their own eyes. Even with all that has taken place in this world, mankind has continually hardened its hearts during the time of the tribulation. Some will come to repentance for their actions, and others will just turn away.

> Galatians 5:19-21 "Now the deeds of the flesh are evident, which are: immorality, impurity, sensuality, 20 idolatry, sorcery, enmities, strife, jealousy, outbursts of anger, disputes, dissensions, factions, 21 envying, drunkenness, carousing, and things like these, of which I forewarn you, just as I have forewarned you, that those who practice such things will not inherit the kingdom of God."

Mankind will not give God the rightful place in their hearts because their hearts are filled with the things that appease their sinful nature. Just as people are today, so they will be in end times.

9

THE ANGEL AND THE SCROLL

REVELATION 10:1-11 "I SAW ANOTHER STRONG ANGEL coming down from heaven, clothed with a cloud; and the rainbow was on his head, and his face was like the sun, and his feet like pillars of fire; 2 and he had in his hand a little scroll, which was open. He placed his right foot on the sea and his left on the land; 3 and he cried out with a loud voice, as when a lion roars; and when he had cried out, the seven peals of thunder uttered their voices. 4 When the seven peals of thunder had spoken, I was about to write; and I heard a voice from heaven, saying, "Seal up the things which the seven peals of thunder have spoken, and do not write them." 5 Then the angel whom I saw standing on the sea and on the land raised his right hand to heaven, 6 and swore by Him who lives forever and ever, who created heaven and the things in it, and the earth and the things in it, and the sea and the things in it, that there will no longer be a delay, 7 but in the days of the voice of the seventh angel, when he is about to sound, then the mystery of God is finished, as He announced to His servants the prophets.8 Then the voice which I heard from heaven,

I heard again speaking with me, and saying, "Go, take the scroll which is open in the hand of the angel who stands on the sea and on the land." 9 And I went to the angel, telling him to give me the little scroll. And he said to me, "Take it and eat it; it will make your stomach bitter, but in your mouth it will be sweet as honey." 10 I took the little scroll from the angel's hand and ate it, and in my mouth it was sweet as honey; and when I had eaten it, my stomach was made bitter. 11 And they said to me, "You must prophesy again concerning many peoples, nations, languages, and kings."

John closed his eyes as if to try and stop all the images that were going through his head. In his mind, he could not understand why the people refused to turn to God. John grew tired of seeing men refuse to repent. I can imagine that He just wanted to grab them and shake them to try and give the message of salvation through Jesus Christ. If only he could talk to them to give them hope, and show them the answer of Jesus, but after all that has occurred if they had not turned to God by now, what would his words do?

In the next moment, John found himself on earth. "A strong angel had come down from heaven, clothed with a cloud; and the rainbow was on his head, and his face was like the sun, and his feet like pillars of fire; in his hand, he carried a little scroll, which was open. He placed his right foot on the sea and his left on the land, and he spoke out with a loud voice." John covered his ears as the sound was so loud as the sound of a roaring lion with thunder crashing in the background. The angel lifted his voice in praise to God raising his hand to heaven saying, "By Him who lives forever and ever, who created heaven and the things in it, and the earth and the things in it, and the sea and the things in it, that there will no longer be a delay," as he shared the mysteries of God.

Just then, John heard a voice from heaven, say "Go, take the scroll which is open in the hand of the angel who stands on the sea and on the land." John slowly approached the angel, taking the scroll in his hand. The angel in his mighty stature looked down at John and said, "Take it and eat it; it will make your stomach bitter, but in your mouth, it will be sweet as honey." John did not understand at first, but who was he not to do as he was commanded. As John ate, the taste of the scroll was like sweet honey from the honeycomb. The taste touched his mouth and brought joy to his lips, as the sweetness of the honey was like nourishment to him. Once the scroll had reached his stomach, his stomach began to churn. John felt sick.

At that moment the voice said to John, "You must prophesy again concerning many peoples, nations, languages, and kings."

As we come to chapter 10 of Revelation it seems like Jesus is giving John a time out from the judgments of Revelation. As John speaks to this mighty angel, the mighty angel has a little book or a scroll in his hand. When John ate the scroll why was it as sweet as honey, but bitter to his stomach? I believe that this little scroll contained the message of God's plan for mankind.

So why was it that John was told to seal up the things which the seven peals of thunder have spoken, and do not write them? This is the only proclamation in Revelation that is sealed up. Everything else has been written in God's Word.

I believe that the reason this message is not written down was that it most likely had to do with the message of the coming of the Savior Jesus in the Millennium Kingdom, and New Jerusalem as our eternal home and dwelling place with God. However, it probably also contains the judgment of Christ on sinners who do not repent and come to Him. We are not told.

If there is something that we need to know, God will reveal it to us. Otherwise, we should trust in His plan and His work in our lives.

10

THE TWO WITNESS AND THE HOLY CITY

REVELATION 11:1-2 "THEN THERE WAS GIVEN TO ME A measuring rod like a staff; and someone said, "Get up and measure the temple of God and the altar, and those who worship in it. 2 Leave out the courtyard which is outside the temple and do not measure it, because it has been given to the nations; and they will trample the holy city for forty-two months."

John who had just been standing with the mighty angel was now transported to Jerusalem. John looked around trying to get his bearing. The hills and the place seemed familiar, but the building looked different. As John continued to look, he now had no question where he was. For most of this life, he had spent time in this place. It was Jerusalem. John sat down looking at the things around him that were much different than before. In the next moment, an angel came up to John and gave him a measuring rod. John was to measure the temple, the altar, and all those who worship in the temple. He was given specific instruction to leave out the courtyard which is outside the temple because it had been given to nations other than the Jewish people. Those who are outside the temple will trample the holy city for forty-two months or three and a half years.

The two earlier Jewish temples were divided into four areas: The first was the sanctuary itself, which only priests could enter. In the second area, the men of Israel could enter. The third area was the court of the women in which Israelite women worshiped God. The last area was the court of the Gentiles. It was here in the court of Gentiles that the moneychangers had set up their booths. John is told that this area has been given over to the nations. (*The Temple* [1] *Illustration on page 173*)

In Revelation 11:1-2, it appears the image describes preservation since the outer court is not measured and is overrun by the Gentiles for 42 months. The Temple, the holy place, and the worshipers are all measured. It might sound odd to measure the worshipers, but the word can mean measure or count.

John's instruction was to measure the first three, thus symbolizing God's interest and protection of the Jewish nation. The old temple had a court in the open air, for the heathens who worshipped the God of Israel.

Why would John have to measure the temple of God? To this day there have been speculations on where the temple actually stood. Many believe that the temple stood in the place, whereas of now, the Muslim Mosque called the Dome of the Rock stands. Both Jews and Muslims have been fighting back and forth for centuries over who owns this ground.

The next time the voice speaks, it has a warning for the inhabitants of Jerusalem; that the Gentile nations will overrun Jerusalem "and the holy city shall they tread under foot forty and two months". We are dealing here with that period that the Lord Jesus spoke of in Luke 21:24 where is says, "and they will fall by the edge of the sword, and will be led captive into all the nations; and Jerusalem will be trampled underfoot by the Gentiles until the times of the Gentiles are fulfilled."

This had been going on before John wrote about his experiences. Jerusalem had been "tread under foot" by four armies: the Romans, Persians, Saracens, and Turks. The severe kind of treading which is spoken of here will not occur until sometime after the seventh angel sounds his trumpet in the second half of the tribulation.

To understand the coming of the temple that is referred to in Revelation 11 you must understand that the temple is not built yet. Even today there is controversy on the exact location of the temple and why it cannot be built. The Jewish people believe that the new temple should be built on the top of the Temple Mount in the Old City of Jerusalem. This is what has caused tension between the Jews and those of the Muslim faith.

If you were to stand on the Mount of Olives today, you would see the Dome of the Rock on the top of the area where people believe the temple would be located. Why do the Jews believe this is where the temple must be built? In the thirteenth century, when the Jews started coming back to Israel, there was a church of the crusaders called the Temple of Domini on the temple mount. Because the Temple of Domini was located on the spot where the Dome of the rock now stands, the Jews believed that this must have been the place where Solomons' Temple was located. But there are not any original historical records for the existence of the temple in the place where the Dome of the Rock now stands.

During the Roman occupancy in Jerusalem, every Roman fort was built close to the dimensions of 1200 x 600 ft. square or rectangular. When the Roman Empire seized Jerusalem, they would have likely made the area of the temple mount the location for their fort due to its position for its defense against invaders. The Roman occupation of the tenth legion, which was at least ten thousand men, occupied Jerusalem. At the time of the Roman occupation, the Romans and the Jews did not mingle together. Every single facet of the Romans' lives, such as housing, markets, and bathhouses would need to be found inside that fort.

Josephus, the first-century Romano-Jewish scholar, and historian said that Fort of Antonio, which is where the Dome of the Rock now stands, is much larger in scope than the Temple of God described to us in Scripture.

Josephus described the fort as being "erected upon a rock of fifty cubits in height" on a "great precipice." It had "all kinds of rooms and other conveniences, such as courts, and places for bathing, and broad spaces for camps, such that it had all the conveniences of cities and seemed like it was composed of several cities." (Josephus: Antiquities of the Jews, Of the War Book V 5 section 8)

Josephus said, from the north side, the fort would block the view of the temple. If the temple was on the Temple Mount, you would have no problem seeing the temple. "And as that hill on which the tower of Antonia stood, was the highest of these three, so did it adjoin to the new city: and was the only place that hindered the sight of the temple on the north." (Antiq. III.6 section 8)

The original temple was located in the northern part of the city of David, right next to the walls of the temple mount, over the Gihon Spring. Within the Temple, a natural spring gushing up gave an abundance of water to the Sanctuary. The only place where this could occur in Jerusalem was over the Gihon Spring.

> Ezekiel 47:1-2 "Then he brought me back to the door of the house; and behold, water was flowing from under the threshold of the house toward the east, for the house faced east. And the water was flowing down from under, from the right side of the house, from south of the altar. 2 And he brought me out by way of the north gate and led me around on the outside to the outer gate, by the way facing east. And behold, water was spurting out from the south side."

The key point here is that if you look at the archaeological evidence of the true location, there is nothing keeping the temple from being built today. The stage is set right now for the work of rebuilding the Temple in Jerusalem.

Every preparation has been made except for the building of the Temple. Even today, at the Institute of Temple Treasures in Jerusalem you can see that they have already made everything that needs to go into this temple in the preparation for the building. They have fashioned all the spoons, goblets, plates, the oil lamps, the showbread table, and more, in the same way the originals were made.

They have made all the wall hangings and cloths just like the originals, and have even dyed them using the same techniques used back in Bible times. Everything is completely ready. All that needs to be done is to build the Temple.

By seeing all the evidence through the Bible and throughout history, this would seem to make it clear that there will be a temple at the time of John's vision.

THE TWO WITNESSES

Revelation 11:3-6 "And I will grant authority to my two witnesses, and they will prophesy for 1,260 days, clothed in sackcloth." 4 These are the two olive trees and the two lampstands that stand before the Lord of the earth. 5 And if anyone wants to harm them, fire flows out of their mouth and devours their enemies; and so if anyone wants to harm them, he must be killed in this way. 6 These have the power to shut up the sky, so that rain will not fall during the days of their prophesying; and they have power over the waters to turn them into blood, and to strike the earth with every plague, as often as they desire."

We are now at the point that three and a half years have passed during the tribulation period and there are three and a half years left to go. God had sent two men who would proclaim His word for 1260 days during the Tribulation. That is 42 months or 3½ years.

After John had completed the measurement, he saw two men standing in the midst of a crowd. It seemed as people from all nations had gathered to hear their message. John heard them speak with bold voices as they declared with confidence the scripture from God's Word. Many people walked away, but some stayed. These men were preaching the gospel. As John was told, "these two men were witnesses of God." Their whole purpose on this earth was to declare the good news of Christ and the glory of God.

These were two men who were filled with the Holy Spirit, speaking the declaration of God to all mankind. It was like they were lampstands, shining in the midst of the darkness of this world with the Holy Spirit filling them as oil fills a lamp. They were shining examples of a changed life. The brilliance of God showed through them as if the light of the sun shines a perfect beam of light through a magnifying glass.

As the two men gave their testimony of God's grace and mercy, the crowd, who stood before the two witnesses separated as a river splitting into two directions. Some men made their way through the crowds of people, carrying pipes, rocks, and swords. As they approached the two witnesses, they hurled violent words, insults, and profanity at the two witnesses. The closer they got, the more the crowd seemed to back away as if something was about to happen. The men started moving closer and closer to the two witnesses. In no time the men were close enough to attack them. The witnesses gazed upon the men and opened their mouths as a great fire flew from their lips. The flames engulfed the men as their whole bodies were covered in fire.

The flames grew with great intensity so that their whole bodies were encompassed with fire. One by one the men dropped to their knees and fell dead at their feet.

John witnessed the power of these men, who by their decrees, stopped the rain from falling upon the earth. They turned the waters into blood and cause the earth to have plagues that had only been seen in the time of Moses. If anyone wanted to harm them, fire flowed out of their mouths and devoured their enemies. These two men have the power to authenticate their mission to unbelieving Israel. These men have miraculous power to bring fire down from heaven and have unlimited authority over the things of this earth, as they are filled with the Holy Spirit, who gives them power. They control rainfall on the earth, and they are able to turn water into blood. These two witnesses are immortal and immune to all attacks until their mission is complete. But who are these two witnesses?

I believe these two men are Moses and Elijah. Look at what we have seen through history. Elijah, through the power of God, shut up the sky so that rain would not fall. God allowed Elijah to call fire down from the sky when he faced the prophets of Baal at Mount Carmel. For Moses, it was the plaques and the turning of water into blood. Also, it seems to me to be almost certain that Elijah is one of the witnesses since it was predicted that he would return.

> Malachi 4:5 "Behold, I am going to send you Elijah the prophet before the coming of the great and terrible day of the Lord."

Moses represents the Law, and Elijah the Prophets. Moses represents those who have died in the Lord, and Elijah those who have not. Moses wrote the Law which anticipated the sacrificial atonement of the Messiah and Elijah was to come to prepare the hearts of the people for the coming of the Lord.

Since we do not know who these two witnesses are we can only speculate. Even though we are not told their identity, the one thing we can be sure of is that God never allows Himself to be without a witness.

The very period of the trampling down of Jerusalem will be the same time of their testimony, i.e., 1260 days. Also remember that there are also 144,000 witnesses who do not have the power of these two men, but still continue the message of God.

Even in the end times the message of God's grace, mercy, and forgiveness still continued to be preached.

THE FACE-OFF

> Revelation 11:7-14 "When they have finished their testimony, the beast that comes up out of the abyss will make war with them, and overcome them and kill them. 8 And their dead bodies will lie on the street of the great city which spiritually is called Sodom and Egypt, where also their Lord was crucified. 9 Those

from the peoples, tribes, languages, and nations will look at their dead bodies for three and a half days, and will not allow their dead bodies to be laid in a tomb. 10 And those who live on the earth will rejoice over them and celebrate; and they will send gifts to one another, because these two prophets tormented those who live on the earth. 11 And after the three and a half days, the breath of life from God came into them, and they stood on their feet; and great fear fell upon those who were watching them.12 And they heard a loud voice from heaven saying to them, "Come up here." And they went up into heaven in the cloud, and their enemies watched them. 13 And at that time there was a great earthquake, and a tenth of the city fell; seven thousand people were killed in the earthquake, and the rest were terrified and gave glory to the God of heaven.14 The second woe has passed; behold, the third woe is coming quickly."

John watched as the crowds dissipated from in front of his eyes, as a group of heavily armed men approached the two witnesses. John readied himself to see the two prophets defend themselves against the armed soldiers, but what happened next is not what John had expected.

The group of armed men slowly moved to one side as a well-dressed man, great in stature, someone who seemed to have great power, distinctly walked to them smiling as he came. The man spoke with elegant words in a welcoming way.

Once reaching the two witnesses, in a split moment, with lightning speed that John had never seen before, the well-dressed man, struck both men, knocking them to the earth. He looked upon the men, with a smile as if to say, "This could have been avoided my friends, for there is only one god and that is me."

John watched as the two men lay on the ground. He could see their heads, which were once still hovering above the ground, finally fall to the dust of the earth. Their eyes slowly closed as their chest fell. They were dead. The well-dressed man dusted off his hands, and then turned to leave, smiling and waving to the people who all cheered with joy for the victory of the man. He turned and left.

The two witnesses were left in the street, dead on the ground. All those who lived on the earth rejoiced over the two witnesses celebrating this victory and the death of the two men. People sent gifts to one another as if it was a celebration of Christmas for the victory of the well-dressed man who was, in fact, the Antichrist.

John stood there in disgust, over the manner in which these men were treated. How could you celebrate? How can you not bury them?

John continued to watch as these men lay dead in the street. He looked up to heaven and back down at the men. John knew that God had a purpose. So, he watched intently at what God was going to do. Would it be lightning upon the people? Would it again be hail mixed with fire and blood? But nothing happened.

After three and a half days, something strange began to happen. These two men who once laid dead in the street started to move. The breath of life from God had come back into them. John watched as they first sat up, then, in the next moment, they stood up dusting themselves off as if nothing had ever happened. The people who had celebrated their death now began to scream in horror.

Many people began to run away, some were in shock at the sight that was before their eyes. John cheered in celebration for God, as a loud and wonderous voice spoke from heaven saying, "Come up here." John watched as the two men began to float as if all gravity had suddenly vanished from around them, as they flew up in the clouds. All those around watched with fear.

Suddenly without warning the earth shook violently, as a great earthquake shook the walls and the buildings of the city. A tenth of the city fell as John watched as the walls and buildings collapsed around him. People screamed and frantically ran to try and hide, to find some safety from the terror that now consumed them. "Seven thousand people were killed in the earthquake, and the rest were terrified and gave glory to the God of heaven. The second woe has passed; behold, the third woe is coming quickly."

THE SEVENTH TRUMPET JUDGEMENT

> Revelation 11:15-19 "Then the seventh angel sounded; and there were loud voices in heaven, saying, "The kingdom of the world has become the kingdom of our Lord and of His Christ; and He will reign forever and ever." 16 And the twenty-four elders, who sit on their thrones before God, fell on their faces and worshiped

God, 17 saying, "We give You thanks, Lord God, the Almighty, the One who is and who was, because You have taken Your great power and have begun to reign. 18 And the nations were enraged, and Your wrath came, and the time came for the dead to be judged, and the time to reward Your bond-servants the prophets and the saints and those who fear Your name, the small and the great, and to destroy those who destroy the earth."19 And the temple of God which is in heaven was opened; and the ark of His covenant appeared in His temple, and there were flashes of lightning and sounds and peals of thunder, and an earthquake, and a great hailstorm."

John was taken back to the throne room of God. The sounds of praise again began to fill his ears. From the moments on earth with the earthquakes and terror to the sounds of peace; the peace that only God gives.

John watched as the last angel who held a trumpet made his way to the throne. He raised the trumpet to his lips and let the sound of the trumpet roar.

At the sound of the trumpet, all voices in heaven opened up in glory as they said, "The kingdom of the world has become the kingdom of our Lord and of His Christ; and He will reign forever and ever." John, then filled in awe at the person of Jesus Christ, bowed with the elders and all who were in heaven.

The sounding of the seventh trumpet signals the long-awaited arrival of the Kingdom of God on earth. This trumpet will be one of the most important announcements in human history. The establishment of the Kingdom of God on earth is the fulfillment of biblical prophecies recorded throughout the Bible. Thus ends the seven trumpet judgments.

In the interpretation of King Nebuchadnezzar's dream from the book of Daniel, God through the prophet Daniel revealed that eventually, a kingdom would arise that would destroy all the human governments that preceded it. Most important, God said that His kingdom "shall never be destroyed ... and it shall stand forever" (Daniel 2:44).

11

THE BATTLE IN HEAVEN

REVELATION 12:1-5 "A GREAT SIGN APPEARED IN HEAVEN: a woman clothed with the sun, and the moon under her feet, and on her head a crown of twelve stars; 2 and she was pregnant and she cried out, being in labor and in pain to give birth.3 Then another sign appeared in heaven: and behold, a great red dragon having seven heads and ten horns, and on his heads were seven crowns. 4 And his tail swept away a third of the stars of heaven and hurled them to the earth. And the dragon stood before the woman who was about to give birth, so that when she gave birth he might devour her Child.5 And she gave birth to a Son, a male, who is going to rule all the nations with a rod of iron; and her Child was caught up to God and to His throne."

As we begin Revelation chapter 12, we are given a glimpse of a scene that shows us a limited edition of the history of the angelic world.

Have you ever been given a backstage pass to a concert? Or maybe you watched a video that explained to you all the things that happened behind the scenes of your favorite movie. When you watch a movie, you are hardly aware of all the activities that happened in the background of the filming. The directors, the producers, the people who are working the cameras, the microphones, the lights, and the special effects crew. So many things happen behind the scenes that we do not see as we watch the movie.

John gives a detailed look at what was happening behind the scenes in heaven. "A great and wondrous sign appeared in heaven: a woman clothed with the sun, with the moon under her feet and a crown of twelve stars on her head."

What was the sign or symbol that John saw? A woman. Now, who did this woman symbolize? Many people believe that this was the Virgin Mary, because the next verse says, "She was pregnant and cried out in pain as she was about to give birth." Is this Mary? Yes, and no. The depiction of the women seen here is a representation of the Jews. John saw that this woman has twelve stars on her head. This is a representation of the twelve's tribes of Israel. Mary, who was a Jew, gave birth to Jesus. The woman is representative of the people of God.

> Galatians 4:4–5 "But when the fullness of the time came, God sent His Son, born of a woman, born under the Law, 5 so that He might redeem those who were under the Law, that we might receive the adoption as sons and daughters."

The very purpose of His coming was to destroy the walls of sin and the law which divide mankind from God and to restore the relationship that was once destroyed by sin.

John describes his vision of what was really happening when Jesus was being born. It was a declaration of war. The devil's forces were in an uproar. This war is very significant and relevant to us in our everyday lives and has changed our future to a great degree. There are no "conscientious objectors" in this war. We are already involved. Paul reminds us that the people of God are involved in spiritual warfare.

> Ephesians 6:12 "For our struggle is not against flesh and blood, but against the rulers, against the powers, against the world forces of this darkness, against the spiritual forces of wickedness in the heavenly places."

Satan's desire was to kill this child before he was even born. Remember when the wise men told King Herod of the foretold birth of the new King? What was Herod's plan? To find this new King and kill Him. This is why Joseph was told by an angel in a dream to escape to Egypt.

As John sees the next part of his vision, we see the adversary of the woman, a dragon.

> Revelation 12:3-4 "Then another sign appeared in heaven: and behold, a great red dragon having seven heads and ten horns, and on his heads were seven crowns. 4 And his tail swept away a third of the stars of heaven and hurled them to the earth."

Here the mortal enemy of the women is Satan, who appears as a dragon. Revelation 12:9 says, "And the great dragon was thrown down, the serpent of old who is called the devil and Satan, who deceives the whole world"

The dragon is described in terms of evil intent, power, wisdom, and authority. We are also told that the dragon's tail "swept away a third of the stars of heaven and hurled them to the earth." At the point of Satan's sin to be greater than God, he led one-third of the angels with him. Today we know them as fallen angels or demons. This battle did not just start at the birth of Jesus, it began when Satan's pride led him to sin.

The book of Isaiah gives us a vivid picture of what happened in heaven and what caused Satan to be kicked out of heaven.

> Isaiah 14:11-15 "Your pride and the music of your harps Have been brought down to Sheol; Maggots are spread out as your bed beneath you And worms are your covering.' 12 How you have fallen from heaven, You star of the morning, son of the dawn! You have been cut down to the earth, You who defeated the nations! 13 But you said in your heart, 'I will ascend to heaven; I will raise my throne above the stars of God, And I will sit on the mount of assembly In the recesses of the north.14 I will ascend above the heights of the clouds; I will make myself like the Most High.'15 Nevertheless you will be brought down to Sheol, To the recesses of the pit."

What was it that caused Satan to be kicked out of heaven? The sin in his heart. Notice in Isaiah 14 the five things that he said,

Isaiah 14:13-14 "But you said in your heart, 'I will ascend to heaven; I will raise my throne above the stars of God, And I will sit on the mount of assembly In the recesses of the north.14 I will ascend above the heights of the clouds; I will make myself like the Most High.'"

- "I will ascend to heaven;" What Satan was inferring here was that he, Satan, would take the place of God.

- "I will raise my throne above the stars of God." Satan wanted to be in charge and rule angels.

- "I will sit on the mount of assembly In the recesses of the north." He wanted to rule over mankind.

- "I will ascend above the heights of the clouds." Satan wanted to be the supreme ruler, to displace God as the Sovereign of the universe.

- "I will make myself like the Most High." Satan wanted nothing more than to be God. He had a power lust.

How could Satan ever believe he could take God's place. Satan was a created being. In Ezekiel 28 look at how Satan was described, what he looks like, and what he did.

Ezekiel 28:12 "… 'This is what the Lord God says: "You had the seal of perfection, Full of wisdom and perfect in beauty. 13 You were in Eden, the garden of God; Every precious stone was your covering: The ruby, the topaz and the diamond; The beryl, the onyx and the jasper; The lapis lazuli, the turquoise and the emerald; And the gold, the workmanship of your settings and sockets, Was in you. On the day that you were created They were prepared. 14 You were the anointed cherub who covers, And I placed you there. You were on the holy mountain of God; You walked in the midst of the stones of fire. 15 You were blameless in your ways From the day you were created Until unrighteousness was found in you.16 By the abundance of your trade You were internally filled with violence, And you sinned; Therefore I have cast you as profane From the mountain of God. And I have destroyed you, you covering cherub, From the midst of the stones of fire. 17 Your heart was haughty because of your beauty; You corrupted your wisdom by reason of your splendor. I threw you to the ground; I put you before kings, That they may see you."

Notice the verse which said, "On the day that you were created". Satan is a created being, but God was never created. He has always existed. He is the sovereign, Almighty God who created all things. How can a created being say that he is greater than God?

Satan was adorned with every precious jewel imaginable. He was the "anointed cherub." The cherub's purpose was to magnify the holiness and power of God. This is one of their main responsibilities throughout the Bible.

The cherubs also served as a visible reminder of the majesty and glory of God and His abiding presence with His people. But Satan's pride led to his sin and one day he will face his punishment for his sin.

Some people have asked the question did God create sin? The answer is absolutely not! God never created sin. Due to our free will, we have a choice. God did not create robots. He created men and angels with the ability to think and reason and to make choices.

Take for instance a parent and their child. A parent can create the situation that makes disobedience possible, but the parent remains innocent if the child sins. For example, if a parent tells his child to clean up his room and the child does not, the child has rebelled and sinned. But the parent is not responsible for the child's sin, nor did he cause the child to sin. The child had a choice to obey or not to obey.

> James 1:13-15 "No one is to say when he is tempted, "I am being tempted by God"; for God cannot be tempted by evil, and He Himself does not tempt anyone. 14 But each one is tempted when he is carried away and enticed by his own lust. 15 Then when lust has conceived, it gives birth to sin; and sin, when it has run its course, brings forth death."

Sin comes by our own choice, whether we choose to obey or disobey God. No one forces that decision on us. We all make the choice to sin on our own. This is true with Satan and the angels that followed him and were kicked out of heaven.

Revelation 12:5 "And she gave birth to a Son, a male, who is going to rule all the nations with a rod of iron; and her Child was caught up to God and to His throne."

This male child was Jesus Christ. Despite Satan's efforts to destroy Israel and the messianic line, Jesus' birth took place as predicted by the prophets. Jesus will rule the nations and will be crowned King over the nations of the world.

Revelation 12:7-9 "And there was war in heaven, Michael and his angels waging war with the dragon. The dragon and his angels waged war, 8 and they did not prevail, and there was no longer a place found for them in heaven. 9 And the great dragon was thrown down, the serpent of old who is called the devil and Satan, who deceives the whole world; he was thrown down to the earth, and his angels were thrown down with him."

John has seen the background of what has happened from history in the war of Satan's plot to destroy God's plan. Has Satan not learned that he cannot stop God from achieving what He wants to do?

There is a great war that has broken out against the angels in heaven. Up to this point every angel including Satan has still been accountable for their actions.

Job 1:6-7 "Now there was a day when the sons of God came to present themselves before the Lord, and Satan also came among them. 7 The Lord said to Satan, "From where do you come?" Satan answered the Lord and said, "From roaming about on the earth and walking around on it."

As the battle begins. Michael, who is the chief angel, brought forth the angels of heaven against Satan, winning the battle and banishing Satan and his angels to never see heaven again.

> Revelation 12:10-12 "Now the salvation, and the power, and the kingdom of our God and the authority of His Christ have come, for the accuser of our brothers and sisters has been thrown down, the one who accuses them before our God day and night. 11 And they overcame him because of the blood of the Lamb and because of the word of their testimony, and they did not love their life even when faced with death.

Even at this point in our lives, we continue to see Satan attacking everything that God has created and trying to destroy the message of Salvation and the work of God.

Satan has never created anything. He only takes what God has created as good and twists it into something evil. When we do fall into temptation through our sinful natures and succumb to sin, Satan stands before God, day and night, accusing the believers of our sin. But God has forgiven us of all our sins and remembers them no more.

Colossians 2:13-15 "And when you were dead in your wrongdoings and the uncircumcision of your flesh, He made you alive together with Him, having forgiven us all our wrongdoings, 14having canceled the certificate of debt consisting of decrees against us, which was hostile to us; and He has taken it out of the way, having nailed it to the cross. 15When He had disarmed the rulers and authorities, He made a public display of them, having triumphed over them through Him."

No matter what Satan tries to accuse the believers of, God stands victorious because "we have overcome because of the blood of the Lamb." We stand blameless before God because our sins have been forgiven.

Romans 8:33-39 "Who will bring charges against God's elect? God is the one who justifies; 34 who is the one who condemns? Christ Jesus is He who died, but rather, was raised, who is at the right hand of God, who also intercedes for us. 35 Who will separate us from the love of Christ? Will tribulation, or trouble, or persecution, or famine, or nakedness, or danger, or sword? 36 Just as it is written: "For Your sake we are killed all day long; We were regarded as sheep to be slaughtered." 37 But in all these things we overwhelmingly conquer through Him who loved us. 38 For I am convinced that neither death, nor life, nor angels, nor principalities, nor things present, nor things to come, nor powers, 39 nor height, nor depth, nor any other created thing will be able to separate us from the love of God that is in Christ Jesus our Lord."

THE ESCAPE OF THE JEWISH BELIEVERS

Revelation 12:12-17 "For this reason, rejoice, you heavens and you who dwell in them. Woe to the earth and the sea, because the devil has come down to you with great wrath, knowing that he has only a short time. And when the dragon saw that he was thrown down to the earth, he persecuted the woman who gave birth to the male Child. 14 But the two wings of the great eagle were given to the woman, so that she could fly into the wilderness to her place, where she was nourished for a time, times, and half a time, away from the presence of the serpent. 15 And the serpent hurled water like a river out of his mouth after the woman, so that he might cause her to be swept away with the flood. 16 But the earth helped the woman, and the earth opened its mouth and drank up the river which the dragon had hurled out of his mouth." 17 "So the dragon was enraged with the woman, and went off to make war with the rest of her children, who keep the commandments of God and hold to the testimony of Jesus."

Satan has come to realize that his time is limited. Now that his access to heaven is at an end, Satan will intensify his efforts against God and mankind, and specifically target Israel. Satan will now try to pour out all his wrath upon the Jewish believers on this earth and will attempt to destroy God's people, "But the two wings of the great eagle were given to the woman, so that she could fly into the wilderness to her place, where she was nourished for a time, times, and half a time, away from the presence of the serpent."

We are told that Satan persecuted the woman. The word "persecuted' means "to chase or to pursue". Satan's persecution of Israel is an attempt to exterminate God's chosen people. Satan knows that his time is short time and so he goes after the believers with great wrath as he intensifies his persecution of them.

The eagle's wings suggest the miraculous swiftness with which God will help them to escape to a place of safety and security for the remaining years of the tribulation, "a time, and times, and half a time." This period is further described as "a thousand two hundred and threescore days" (Revelation 12:6), or "forty and two months" (Revelation 11:2; 13:5). The phrase "time, and times, and half a time" equals three-and-one-half years. It is the last three and a half years of the tribulation period.

> Revelation 12:15-17 "And the serpent hurled water like a river out of his mouth after the woman, so that he might cause her to be swept away with the flood. 16 But the earth helped the woman, and the earth opened its mouth and drank up the river which the dragon had

hurled out of his mouth. 17 So the dragon was enraged with the woman, and went off to make war with the rest of her children, who keep the commandments of God and hold to the testimony of Jesus."

Furious at the loss of his battle in heaven, Satan focuses his attention on the believers on earth by sending the armies of the Antichrist after the believers of God. This symbol of water that is hurled at the woman, is not physical water, but something that would cause her destruction, an army. As the army goes after the woman, God provided a place of protection to keep her safe from the armies of Satan. I believe this place is called Petra.

Petra is a historic and archaeological city in southern Jordan. It is located in a basin with Mount Seir and is totally surrounded by mountains and cliffs. The only way in and out of the city is through a narrow passageway that extends for a mile and can only be negotiated by foot or by horseback. This means the city is easy to defend.

Petra is shaped in a way that leaves it protected on all sides except through a narrow passage that is only ten to fourteen feet wide, making it impossible for an entire army to get into at one time. Petra also was created with its own water system and aqueducts. Excavations of the city of Petra have demonstrated that it has the ability to control the water supply that leads to the rise of the desert city, creating an artificial oasis. The area is visited by flash floods, but archaeological evidence shows that the city of Petra controlled these floods by the use of dams, cisterns, and water conduits. This will not only give them a safe place to be, but the water to survive.

Matthew 24:15-16 "Therefore when you see the abomination of desolation which was spoken of through Daniel the prophet, standing in the holy place let the reader understand 16 then those who are in Judea must flee to the mountains."

Scripture does not say that the rock-hewn city of Petra will be that place. It could be, but we just simply do not know. Whatever the place of safety is, it will provide sustenance for the escapees for 1,260 days.

12

The Antichrist and the False Prophet

Revelation 13:1-10 "And the dragon stood on the sand of the seashore. Then I saw a beast coming up out of the sea, having ten horns and seven heads, and on his horns were ten crowns, and on his heads were blasphemous names. 2 And the beast that I saw was like a leopard, and his feet were like those of a bear, and his mouth like the mouth of a lion. And the dragon gave him his power and his throne, and great authority. 3 I saw one of his heads as if it had been fatally wounded, and his fatal wound was healed. And the whole earth was amazed and followed after the beast; 4 they worshiped the dragon because he gave his authority to the beast; and they worshiped the beast, saying, "Who is like the beast, and who is able to wage war with him?" 5 A mouth was given to him speaking arrogant words and blasphemies, and authority to act for forty-two months was given to him. 6 And he opened his mouth in blasphemies against God, to blaspheme His name and His tabernacle, that is, those who dwell in heaven.7 It was also given to him to make war with the saints and to overcome them, and authority was given to him over every tribe, people, language, and nation. 8 All who live on the earth will worship him, everyone whose name has not been written since the foundation of the world in the book of life of the Lamb who has been slaughtered. 9 If anyone has an ear, let him hear. 10 If anyone is destined for captivity, to captivity he goes; if anyone kills with the sword, with the sword he must be killed. Here is the perseverance and the faith of the saints."

Satan stood posed behind his chosen man determining the fate of all who failed to recognize God as their Savior. No ordinary man would do.

It had to be someone who was well-spoken. It had to be a man of power, and a man of great charisma who would fulfill the position as Satan's puppet. The Antichrist's main purpose is to acquire power and turn people away from God, directing worship toward himself. He will be Satan's tool for corrupting the world and turning people away from God.

John saw this man, who was the Antichrist, leading the kings of this world, as if they were at his beck and call. John counted only ten kings, presidents, prime ministers, or leaders of this world who were still left. It was through these men that the Antichrist made the world bow to his commands.

John compared the characteristics of the Antichrist to animals that he had seen in the wild. The Antichrist was like a leopard, swift in speed that would accomplish Satan's will upon the world. His feet were like those of a bear, strong and powerful. Because of his strength he had the power over the world to accomplish what he wanted. His mouth was like the mouth of a lion. When he spoke, the world listened and trembled in fear. Behind this man, stood Satan, who gave him the power over the world, giving him everything his heart desired and more.

The Antichrist was portrayed as the savior, the new so-called Christ. His plan was to bring people under his salvation, not through salvation, but through his conquering. The Antichrist in all ways tried to imitate Jesus Christ, attempting to prove himself to be the real messiah that people waited for.

The Antichrist even acclaimed glory that he himself had died and had risen from the dead. This amazed the people of the world and the whole earth followed after the beast, who seemed to have the power over death. In celebration, the followers of the Antichrist worshiped him and Satan who had given him the power.

The people worshipped and praised his name saying, "Who is like the beast, and who is able to wage war with him?"

He will hold the power of this world and he will lead the people astray. Who was like him? As he proclaimed himself as god, and spoke arrogant words and blasphemies, with authority to act for forty-two months or three and half years. The Antichrist will curse any other gods who claimed to be above him. He will hold the power and reign over this earth, as he claims that he is the one true god. He will lead everyone in worship to himself. For whoever will not worship him and recognize him as god, will be sentenced to death.

The Antichrist, like Satan, will be a great blasphemer. A blasphemer is one who curses God, denies the true God, and sets up himself or others as god. The Antichrist will blaspheme the very name of God by taking it for himself. He will speak blasphemy against God's tabernacle, denying the church which had been caught up to God before any of this began. He will deny God's very existence. This will only go on for 1260 days and then the end will come. The Antichrist may take the physical life of a believer, but he cannot destroy a believer's saving faith and eternal life.

THE FALSE PROPHET

Revelation 13:11-18 "Then I saw another beast coming up out of the earth; and he had two horns like a lamb, and he spoke as a dragon. 12 He exercises all the authority of the first beast in his presence. And he makes the earth and those who live on it worship the first beast, whose fatal wound was healed. 13 He performs great signs, so that he even makes fire come down out of the sky to the earth in the presence of people. 14 And he deceives those who live on the earth because of the signs which it was given him to perform in the presence of the beast, telling those who live on the earth to make an image to the beast who had the wound of the sword and has come to life. 15 And it was given to him to give breath to the image of the beast, so that the image of the beast would even speak and cause all who do not worship the image of the beast to be killed. 16 And he causes all, the small and the great, the rich and the poor, and the free and the slaves, to be given a mark on their right hands or on their foreheads, 17 and he decrees that no one will be able to buy or to sell, except the one who has the mark, either the name of the beast or the number of his name. 18 Here is wisdom. Let him who has understanding calculate the number of the beast, for the number is that of a man; and his number is six hundred and sixty-six."

Next to the Antichrist stood a man in high stature. He had position and power, but not like that of the Antichrist. This man was no king, no head of state, not a president, but given the same honor as the Antichrist. When this man spoke, his words were elegant and peaceful. His words seemed to be sweet, but filled with blasphemy at the same time. This man said nothing of himself, but only gave praise and honor to the Antichrist.

As this man spoke, elegant words rang from his mouth, honoring the man who has given the people new life here in this world. He would say that the Antichrist has saved people from their worries, provided for their needs, and given them new hope. He would proclaim that the reason they honor and pay tribute to this man is that he is god.

This man who spoke was a false prophet. He fed lies to the people and caused them to put their hope and life in the beast, the one who is called the Antichrist. Great honor was given to the Antichrist, who had died and come back to life. The people celebrated the Antichrist and honored him with a great and wonderous statue. This was no ordinary statue. It seemed as if it really was the Antichrist. The statue moved as if it was a man and spoke words of peace and hope, of salvation, and life. The people not only honored the Antichrist, but his statue as well.

The false prophet declared that everyone was to honor the Antichrist as their god. Each person was to show reverence and respect by bowing before him. By the command of the false prophet, everyone was to receive the Antichrist name or his number, 666, written on their forehead or on the back of their right hands. By doing this the Antichrist would provide for the people, allowing them to buy and sell in peace. He would make provisions for them, and they would be free from worry because he would provide and protect them.

The people began to cheer and rejoice in their savior the Antichrist. People came from far and wide to receive the mark of the beast in a joyous celebration by honoring their god. How could these people be so easily fooled? There is only one God!

> Revelation 13:6-8 "And he opened his mouth in blasphemies against God, to blaspheme His name and His tabernacle, that is, those who dwell in heaven.7 It was also given to him to make war with the saints and to overcome them, and authority was given to him over every tribe, people, language, and nation. 8 All who live on the earth will worship him, everyone whose name has not been written since the foundation of the world in the book of life of the Lamb who has been slaughtered."

The Antichrist will be over every organization in the end times, and will ultimately grow in power through personal charm and increasing use of force. He will disguise his true motives in the beginning and greatly appeal to the masses. The Antichrist will be given full authority over the earth. He will control everything, and he will even have absolute power over the world's economy. Whoever does not accept his mark and pledge total allegiance to him will not be able to buy, sell, or even eat to survive. This mark will be proof of a person's loyalty to the Antichrist.

In the end times, the Antichrist will have a one-world economy, which means that there will someday be a world ID mark, which will be the mark of the beast and there will be nothing you can do without it. To be under the Antichrist's control means that not only will he have a one-world currency and one-world government, but he will also create a one-world religion in his worship.

Increasingly, religion will be seen as one of the major sources of conflict in the world. Even today, religious differences seem to contribute to the conflicts raging in the world. As we march toward the end, there will be a growing call to unite all religions into one, under the guise of attempting to bring peace and unite the world.

In February 2019. Pope Francis urged Iraq's Muslims, and Christians to work together to unite for peace. Pope Francis' traveled to the original homeland of the Islamic faith and joined eminent Muslims, Jews, and other Christian clerics in an appeal for communal coexistence.

In our society today we face Pluralism. It is the idea that there are many ways to think of God. Have you not seen the bumper stickers that say, COEXIST? This idea of pluralism says, that no one has the right to exclusive truth claims about God. We know Acts 4:12 says "And there is salvation in no one else; for there is no other name under heaven that has been given among mankind by which we must be saved."

We cannot give up the truth in order to just get along. We must respect everyone and recognize that each person has the right to choose whether they accept or reject the truth, but we cannot give up our belief that "there is one God and one mediator between God and men, the man Christ Jesus" (1 Timothy 2:5). To say that the God we worship is the same as Allah, Krishna, or any other god is ludicrous and a denial of the true faith.

In the end times Satan, the Antichrist, and False Prophet will unite in a desperate attempt to establish their own government and overthrow the kingdom of God, but their efforts will ultimately fail.

13

The Redeemed

Revelation 14:1-5 "Then I looked, and behold, the Lamb was standing on Mount Zion, and with Him 144,000 who had His name and the name of His Father written on their foreheads. 2 And I heard a voice from heaven, like the sound of many waters and like the sound of loud thunder, and the voice which I heard was like the sound of harpists playing on their harps. 3 And they sang a new song before the throne and before the four living creatures and the elders; and no one was able to learn the song except the 144,000 who had been purchased from the earth. 4 These are the ones who have not defiled themselves with women, for they are celibate. These are the ones who follow the Lamb wherever He goes. These have been purchased from mankind as first fruits to God and to the Lamb. 5 And no lie was found in their mouths; they are blameless."

John found himself being led to Mount Zion, in the city of David, which he knew all too well. The celebration here was much different than the place he had previously found himself near the Antichrist.

In Revelation 14 we have rejoicing and a celebration, not for the Antichrist, but a celebration for Jesus. There on top of the Mount was Jesus was surrounded by the 144,000 missionaries who had gone out to preach His message of salvation and hope. They had come back to Jesus undefiled and holy before the Lord.

The beautiful music from heaven rained down upon the earth in a sweet and melodious melody to Jesus. The 144,000 sang the most beautiful song to Jesus, a song which John had never heard. Such beauty, such marvelous words. The praise of their voices lifted up to the heavens in celebration of Jesus.

This was not a song of their accomplishments, but the praise and worship of Christ. The only words they gave were honor to the King.

> John 16:33 "These things I have spoken to you so that in
> Me you may have peace. In the world you have tribulation,
> but take courage; I have overcome the world."

The 144,000 seen here are the same 144,000 Jewish believers that were sealed in Revelation 7. There, before the trials of the tribulation got too intense, God set aside 144,000 Jewish believers for Himself. He sealed them with a special mark on their foreheads. He wrote His own name on them to show the world that they belonged to Him and to protect them from the evil one.

For the 144,000, this was uniquely their song. None of the angels could sing it because none of them had experienced what they experienced. No angel has been "redeemed from the earth;" No angel had been purchased out of slavery.

This is special for us. This is our story too. We were wasting away in sin, eaten up by our self-indulgence, and carrying the scars of our sin. Our Heavenly Father came along, laid His hand upon our lives, and said, "This is my child." Then he paid a high price to rescue us from our sin. He let His only Son suffer and die on a cross to pay the price of our redemption. Now we, who put our trust in Christ, belong to Him.

> 1 Peter 1:18-19 "knowing that you were not redeemed with perishable things like silver or gold from your futile way of life inherited from your forefathers, 19 but with precious blood, as of a lamb unblemished and spotless, the blood of Christ."

They are transformed, men and women who were separated unto Him. They are clearly born again. "No lie was found in their mouths; they are blameless," i.e., they are without blemish. They have been cleansed and changed by grace, just as we also have been, if we know the Lord.

Jude 1:24 tells us, that true believers will now be presented before God's presence "without fault and with great joy," It is the same with these redeemed Jews who recognize their once-crucified Messiah and now follow him faithfully. The whole picture of the 144,000 is purity in contrast with those who dwell on the earth, and those who glory in the worship of a false god and false ideas, believing the lie. These 144,000 people kept themselves pure for God.

14

THE DOOM FOR WORSHIPERS
OF THE BEAST

REVELATION 14:6-13 "AND I SAW ANOTHER ANGEL flying in midheaven with an eternal gospel to preach to those who live on the earth, and to every nation, tribe, language, and people; 7 and he said with a loud voice, "Fear God and give Him glory, because the hour of His judgment has come; worship Him who made the heaven and the earth, and sea and springs of waters." 8 And another angel, a second one, followed, saying, "Fallen, fallen is Babylon the great, she who has made all the nations drink of the wine of the passion of her sexual immorality. 9 Then another angel, a third one, followed them, saying with a loud voice, "If anyone worships the beast and his image, and receives a mark on his forehead or on his hand, 10 he also will drink of the wine of the wrath of God, which is mixed in full strength in the cup of His anger; and he will be tormented with fire and brimstone in the presence of the holy angels and in the presence of the Lamb. 11 And the smoke of their torment ascends forever and ever;

they have no rest day and night, those who worship the beast and his image, and whoever receives the mark of his name." 12 Here is the perseverance of the saints who keep the commandments of God and their faith in Jesus.13 And I heard a voice from heaven, saying, "Write: 'Blessed are the dead who die in the Lord from now on!'" "Yes," says the Spirit, "so that they may rest from their labors, for their deeds follow with them."

Revelation 14:7 "and he said with a loud voice, "Fear God and give Him glory, because the hour of His judgment has come; worship Him who made the heaven and the earth, and sea and springs of waters."

This is a demand or command to all people. It also is an announcement of judgment. This is bad news for the wicked but good news for the people of God. A day is coming when good meets evil; right meets wrong; light meets darkness, and it's going to be a horrific battle, but we know the end of the story. God has revealed it to us, good will reign triumphantly for all eternity. As the second angel is heard, the time is drawing near towards the end. ""Fallen, fallen is Babylon the great, she who has made all the nations drink of the wine of the passion of her sexual immorality."

This is the first mention in Revelation of "Babylon the Great." The great city Babylon, which is the worldly system of power of the Antichrist, will move onto center stage in chapters 17 and 18. The picture is given of a woman who rides the beast. Babylon refers to the entire power of the Antichrist. Babylon is at the heart of the antichristian kingdom, as Jerusalem was the heart of Israel. Through the Antichrist and the false prophet, this kingdom enticed the nations to drink the wine of her adulteries, and worship the beast. But the kingdom of the Antichrist, and the great Babylon are about to fall. This is good news for the people of God who had been persecuted by her, but bad news for everyone who followed the Antichrist.

The idea and wording of "Fallen, fallen is Babylon the great, she who has made all the nations drink of the wine of the passion of her sexual immorality" corresponds with Isaiah 21:9, "Babylon is fallen, is fallen," where it relates to idolatry. Jeremiah 51:7-8 is where we obtain the picture of her making the earth drunk with her ideas. The doom of this great city, with all it represents of pride and rebellion, has drawn on itself God's wrath because of its idolatry and sexual misbehavior. The time of final judgment is now fast approaching. Let all those who enjoyed the pleasures of Babylon drink the wine of God's wrath.

As the second angel announced the enemy's defeat, now we have a warning by a third angel.

The last angel's message is "If anyone worships the beast and his image, and receives a mark on his forehead or on his hand, he also will drink of the wine of the wrath of God, which is mixed in full strength in the cup of His anger; and he will be tormented with fire and brimstone in the presence of the holy angels and in the presence of the Lamb. And the smoke of their torment ascends forever and ever; they have no rest day and night, those who worship the beast and his image, and whoever receives the mark of his name."

The messages of the three angels sum up the history of the world for those who dwell on the earth. First, is God's call to the world.

Second, the Antichrist, who will deceive the nations is now fallen. And third, the final doom of all those who have chosen to follow the Antichrist.

The prime reference is as a warning against submission to any false religion or secularism for whatever reason and especially to the final Antichrist depicted by the beast from the abyss.

This last scene in Revelation 14 is a judgment scene; the faithful from the unfaithful. This will be a time of joy for Christians who have been persecuted and martyred because they will receive their own long-awaited reward. Christians should not fear the Last Judgment. Jesus said, John 5:24 "Truly, truly, I say to you, the one who hears My word, and believes Him who sent Me, has eternal life, and does not come into judgment, but has passed out of death into life."

THE HARVESTING

Revelation 14:14-20 "Then I looked, and behold, a white cloud, and sitting on the cloud was one like a son of man, with a golden crown on His head and a sharp sickle in His hand. 15 And another angel came out of the temple, calling out with a loud voice to Him who sat on the cloud, "Put in your sickle and reap, for the hour to reap has come, because the harvest of the earth is ripe." 16 Then He who sat on the cloud swung His sickle over the earth, and the earth was reaped.17 And another angel came out of the temple which is in heaven, and he also had a sharp sickle. 18 Then another angle, the one who has power over fire, came out from the altar; and he called with a loud voice to him who had the sharp sickle, saying, "Put in your sharp sickle and gather the clusters from the vine of the earth, because her grapes are ripe." 19 So the angel swung his sickle to the earth and gathered the clusters from the vine of the earth, and threw them into the great wine press of the wrath of God. 20 And the wine press was trampled outside the city, and blood came out from the wine press, up to the horses' bridles, for a distance of 1,600 stadia."

It is a time another great judgment by God. At this point in John's vision in Revelation 14, this place is referred to as Babylon, the place of the Antichrist domain. It is compared to wheat on a threshing floor that is about to be trampled as the harvest is about to begin.

This judgment will be upon the wicked nations who have followed Antichrist. The increasing corruption and rottenness in the earth are objectionable to a holy God. Man cannot continue as he is without the interruption of divine judgment. It is the earth that is reaped because this is where men dwell and where they have perpetuated their evil works.

Obeying the command, the angel with the sickle swung it across the earth and gathered its grapes. This is a picture of the unbelievers who will receive punishment into the great winepress of God's wrath. They will be cut down from the face of the earth.

A winepress was a large vat or trough where grapes would be collected and then smashed. The juice would flow out of a duct that led into a large holding vat. This symbolism is the same for the unbelievers who are collected and trampled in the winepress outside the city. The judgment symbolized here is also very terrible. "So the angel swung his sickle to the earth and gathered the clusters from the vine of the earth, and threw them into the great winepress of the wrath of God. And the winepress was trampled outside the city, and blood came out from the winepress, up to the horses' bridles, for a distance of 1,600 stadia." One stadia is equal to 600 feet. As God pours his wrath out on the followers of the Antichrist the final blood river that will occur from all the dead bodies from the Battle of Armageddon will be approximately 186 miles long, with a depth of four feet, the average height of a horse's bridle.

The average adult body will have approximately 1.2-1.5 gallons (or 10 units) of blood in their body. Imagine the number of people who will come against God in the final battle in order to fulfill the depth and length of this river of blood. It will be a pool of blood whose depth was enough to reach the height of a horse's bridles. The greatest concern here is not the exact distance; it is the immeasurable extent of God's judgment falling on those who refuse to believe.

God has given man every chance and has done everything needed for mankind's salvation. He has sent prophet after prophet to get men to turn to Him. He has revealed His way through His Word, the Bible. Most of all He has given His Son, Jesus Christ so that we can be saved. What we need to know and what we must never forget is that God is not only perfect in love, but He is also perfect in His justice. In His perfect love, He sent His son, Jesus Christ, to die for our sins and reconcile us back unto Himself. In His perfect justice, He will pour out His wrath upon those who refuse to believe and repent.

15

THE LAST SEVEN

REVELATION 15:1-4 "THEN I SAW ANOTHER SIGN IN heaven, great and marvelous, seven angels who had seven plagues, which are the last, because in them the wrath of God is finished.2 And I saw something like a sea of glass mixed with fire, and those who were victorious over the beast and his image and the number of his name, standing on the sea of glass, holding harps of God. 3 And they sang the song of Moses, the bond-servant of God, and the song of the Lamb, saying, "Great and marvelous are Your works, Lord God, the Almighty; Righteous and true are Your ways, King of the nations! 4 Who will not fear You, Lord, and glorify Your name? For You alone are holy; For all the nations will come and worship before You, For Your righteous acts have been revealed.""

John stood in heaven before the throne of God as he watched the angels that once stood with the trumpets of God depart from the altar. John looked intently at the empty space, which had brought such terrible judgment, now sit dormant. John turned to gaze upon the realm of heaven around him. As he turned he saw a multitude of people, who began to sing in worship to the Lord. The song rang out from their lips a melody of glory and honor and praise. "Great and marvelous are Your works, Lord God, the Almighty; Righteous and true are Your ways, King of the nations! Who will not fear You, Lord, and glorify Your name? For You alone are holy; For all the nations will come and worship before You, For Your righteous acts have been revealed."

The song resonated in John's ears thinking of the victory of the lamb, the glory of His name, and the joy that brought hope to those who believe. I can just imagine John beginning to repeat the words to himself as tears began to flow from his eyes.

It is you oh God, who is glorious. It is you oh God, who is marvelous. You are worthy, my king. The sweet melody brought joy to John's heart and an overwhelming desire to praise the King. You are worthy, you are worthy, my Savior and my God.

> Revelation 15:5-8 "After these things I looked, and the temple of the tabernacle of testimony in heaven was opened, 6 and the seven angels who had the seven plagues came out of the temple, clothed in linen, clean and bright, and their chests wrapped with golden sashes. 7 And one of the four living creatures gave the seven angels seven golden bowls full of the wrath of God, who lives forever and ever. 8 And the temple was filled with smoke from the glory of God and from His power; and no one was able to enter the temple until the seven plagues of the seven angels were finished."

As John finished his worship, he opened his eyes to see that the area where the angels who once held the trumpets, were now being replaced by angels, who awaited the next seven judgments to be declared by God.

One of the angels who worship by the throne of God came, carrying golden bowls. Smoke seemed to fill the temple, honoring God's glory and power as the last judgments were now about to begin.

THE FIRST BOWL JUDGEMENT

> Revelation 16:1-2 "Then I heard a loud voice from the temple, saying to the seven angels, "Go and pour out on the earth the seven bowls of the wrath of God." 2 So the first angel went and poured out his bowl on the earth; and a harmful and painful sore afflicted the people who had the mark of the beast and who worshiped his image."

A voice rang out announcing the final judgment of God's wrath upon the earth. The first angel, carrying the golden bowl, poured out his bowl on the earth. Those who had taken the mark of the beast were brought to instant pain, as sores began to cover their whole body from the top of their heads to the bottom of the soles of their feet.

As God pours out His wrath, it is upon those who choose to reject the warning in chapter 14. This judgment is no longer trying to bring people to repentance; it is to bring judgment and suffering to those on this earth who had received the mark of the beast and denied God. The Bible no longer gives an indication that salvation continues to be offered for those who had taken the mark of the beast. They had made their decision to deny God and follow after the Antichrist. They had blasphemed God by practicing idolatry and would now pay the price.

The term for the "sores" in Revelation comes from the Greek word "helkos", (hell-kos), which can refer to an ulcer or abscess. This is not a minor rash. The idea here is infectious boils all over the body. A boil is an infection in the skin. As it grows, its center fills with pus, causing intense pain in the surrounding area of the boil. The pain of these sores will radiate throughout the infected bodies. There will be no way to find any comfort from these festering sores. If you stand, it hurts, if you sit, it hurts, if you try to lay down, it causes severe pain. Every infected area of the body that comes into contact with any surface will cause intense pain. It will be an intense pain like having a metal nail driven into the skin. These sores will have a crippling effect on all who bear the mark of the beast. There will be no rest, there will be no comfort, just a constant pain without any possibility of relief.

With all the destruction of the world, I believe that there are no more hospitals, medications, or pain relievers of any kind. There will be nothing to escape the intensity of this pain.

THE SECOND BOWL JUDGEMENT

> Revelation 16:3 "The second angel poured out his bowl into the sea, and it became blood like that of a dead man; and every living thing in the sea died."

Each bowl has almost the same effect as the corresponding plague, even the hardening of those on whom they fall, for they are far from being brought to repentance by them (Revelation 16:9). The plagues of Egypt came quickly one after another, so it would seem that the pouring out of these bowls would occur in the same manner.

The second angel pours out his bowl on the sea. It turns into blood like that of a dead man and every living thing in the sea dies. Imagine what that will be like. All living creatures in the seas die. Think of the unbearable stench and the potential for disease. This judgment will interfere with commercial shipping on the seas. It will destroy what is left of the fishing industry and the death of all living sea creatures.

THE THIRD BOWL JUDGEMENT

Revelation 16:4-7 "Then the third angel poured out his bowl into the rivers and the springs of waters; and they became blood. 5 And I heard the angel of the waters saying, "Righteous are You, the One who is and who was, O Holy One, because You judged these things; 6 for they poured out the blood of saints and prophets, and You have given them blood to drink. They deserve it." 7 And I heard the altar saying, "Yes, Lord God, the Almighty, true and righteous are Your judgments."

The second and third bowls were poured out onto every water source on earth. Everywhere you looked, the water was now blood. It may seem as if the earth was bleeding to death. The sea and every freshwater source were now destroyed. Not only are the people, who bear the mark of the beast, in constant pain and torture from the sores, they now are slowly dying of dehydration.

A human can go without food for about three weeks, but would typically only last three to four days without water. Without enough water, your kidneys cannot adequately flush the waste and toxins from your blood. Eventually, your kidneys will cease to function and the rest of your organs will stop. Dehydration happens quickly, causing extreme thirst, fatigue, and ultimately, organ failure, and death. A person may go from feeling thirsty and slightly sluggish on the first day with no water to having organ failure by the third day.

THE FOURTH BOWL JUDGEMENT

> Revelation 16:8-9 "And the fourth angel poured out his bowl upon the sun, and it was given power to scorch people with fire. 9 And the people were scorched with fierce heat; and they blasphemed the name of God who has the power over these plagues, and they did not repent so as to give Him glory."

Imagine for a moment that any person who was exposed to the sun's rays for one second would get an instantaneous third-degree burn. I imagine this is what is happening with this judgment upon the earth.

Right now on the earth, we have a protective layer around the earth called the ozone layer. The ozone layer is made up of ozone gas that acts as a shield encircling the earth to protect us from most of the incoming UV radiation from the sun and protect life from DNA-damaging radiation.

Now the impact of this judgment is far worse than removing the ozone layer, it would be as if the sun's rays would burn any exposed part of a body in an instant.

On a normal summer's day, you can get a sunburn in as little as five minutes. The signs of sunburn can start to appear in as little as 11 minutes and skin can turn red within 2 to 6 hours of being burnt. It will continue to develop for the next 24 to 72 hours, and depending on the severity, it can take days or weeks to heal. Sunburns will become worse with more exposure to UV rays. In this judgment the sun would have the ability to scorch you immediately.

The people despised God so much that they did not repent. "And the people were scorched with fierce heat; and they blasphemed the name of God who has the power over these plagues, and they did not repent so as to give Him glory." Their refusal to acknowledge God showed the hardness of their heart.

THE FIFTH BOWL JUDGEMENT

> Revelation 16:10-11 "And the fifth angel poured out his bowl on the throne of the beast, and his kingdom became darkened; and they gnawed their tongues because of pain, 11 and they blasphemed the God of

heaven because of their pain and their sores; and they did not repent of their deeds."

There is a sense in which the fourth and fifth bowl judgments offer the wicked a preview of hell. In the fourth bowl judgment, the sun scorches the beast's worshipers. In the fifth bowl judgment, the beast's kingdom is plunged into darkness. Hell is described in terms of fiery torment.

It is "the lake of fire and sulfur" (Rev. 20:10); "the lake of fire" (Rev. 20:14-15); and "the lake that burns with fire and sulfur" (Rev. 21:8). Jesus describes hell as "the eternal fire prepared for the Devil and his angels" (Matt. 25:41). Hell is where "the fire is not quenched" (Mark 9:48). It is a place where the rich man is "in agony in this flame" (Luke 16:24).

Jesus also describes separation from God as "outer darkness" where "there will be weeping and gnashing of teeth" (Matt. 22:13; 25:30). Flame and darkness are fitting terms for God's judgment upon sin and sinners. Fire consumes filth, and darkness describes banishment from the presence of God, who is light (1 John 1:5). Those who persist in their love of darkness will ultimately receive what they desire: eternal separation from God in outer darkness. The fifth bowl judgment seems to offer a foretaste of the blackness of hell.

With the coming of this judgment the people were already in such pain, and torment and now they are basked in darkness. This fear has crippled them as they now begin to gnaw their tongues in fear and pain. The Greek word is masaomai (mas-sah'-o-mah), meaning to chew, consume, eat, or devour. This judgment takes all light out of the

147

Beast's kingdom. There is no good; no justice; no mercy; no kindness, nothing of Jesus is left.

They may be gnawing their tongues because of the extreme cold caused by the extended darkness, the sores from the first bowl judgment, the dehydration or the severe burns sustained during the fourth bowl judgment, or a combination of all four factors.

The followers of the Antichrist are now fully in darkness, and they gnaw their tongues, due to the anguish and distress, and their anger. And John says, "Still they would not repent!" Instead, they gnawed their tongues in agony and cursed God even more.

THE SIXTH BOWL JUDGMENT

Revelation 16:12-16 "The sixth angel poured out his bowl on the great river, the Euphrates; and its water was dried up, so that the way would be prepared for the kings from the east.13 And I saw coming out of the mouth of the dragon, and out of the mouth of the beast, and out of the mouth of the false prophet, three unclean spirits like frogs; 14 for they are spirits of demons, performing signs, which go out to the kings of the entire [g]world, to gather them together for the war of the great day of God, the Almighty. 15 ("Behold, I am coming like a thief. Blessed is the one who stays awake and keeps his clothes, so that he will not walk about naked and people will not see his shame.") 16

And they gathered them together to the place which in Hebrew is called Har-Magedon."

Revelation 16 describes the end of the age and the last battle that will be fought. The followers of the Antichrist will come together to fight God. I know that sounds crazy. Who can fight God?

> 1 Chronicles 29:11-13 "Yours, Lord, is the greatness, the power, the glory, the victory, and the majesty, indeed everything that is in the heavens and on the earth; Yours is the dominion, Lord, and You exalt Yourself as head over all. 12 Both riches and honor come from You, and You rule over all, and in Your hand is power and might; and it lies in Your hand to make great and to strengthen everyone. 13 Now therefore, our God, we thank You, and praise Your glorious name."

"The sixth angel poured out his bowl on the great river, the Euphrates; and its water was dried up so that the way would be prepared for the kings from the east." The final battle will not take place yet, but soon as the kings of this earth are preparing to come against God in Revelation 19. The sixth bowl judgment will dry up that river to make way for the "kings of the east." Those "kings from the east" will march a sizable army across to battle with Jesus, the King of kings.

The forces of the Antichrist are gathering together to prepare for the battle of Armageddon. The name Armageddon transliterates (translates) the Hebrew words Har-Maggedon, meaning "the hill or mount of

Megiddo. The ancient city of Megiddo is located between Galilee and Samaria, close to the Valley of Jezreel. This section is called the Manasseh mountains and they continue towards the great depression of the Jordan Valley. It is here that the final battle will take place.

THE SEVENTH BOWL JUDGEMENT

> Revelation 16:17-21 "Then the seventh angel poured out his bowl upon the air, and a loud voice came out of the temple from the throne, saying, "It is done." 18 And there were flashes of lightning and sounds and peals of thunder; and there was a great earthquake, such as there had not been since mankind came to be upon the earth, so great an earthquake was it, and so mighty. 19 The great city was split into three parts, and the cities of the nations fell. Babylon the great was remembered in the sight of God, to give her the cup of the wine of His fierce wrath. 20 And every island fled, and no mountains were found. 21 And huge hailstones, weighing about a talent each, came down from heaven upon people; and people blasphemed God because of the plague of the hail, because the hailstone plague was extremely severe."

John saw the last angel as he stood at the altar before the Lord. It was the last of the judgments of God upon this earth.

God is holy, just, and righteous, as well as loving. God can never be one without the other. God cannot be one attribute and contradict another. He always has to be true to who He is, and so He must destroy the wicked.

John watched as the seventh angel poured out his bowl in the atmosphere and the earth shook. This was the greatest earthquake that the earth has ever seen. All the cities of the world began to fall. All high mountain ranges began to dissolve into the earth and all islands disappeared. John watched as even his beloved Jerusalem was divided into three parts. John knew that the pouring out of this bowl was an act of divine wrath and vengeance. The effects of this bowl would not only reach to the kings of the earth and their armies, who would be slain, but their flesh would be given to the fowls of the air. The great city of the Antichrist was destroyed as Babylon the Great received its final judgment.

What was the punishment for blasphemy against God in the Bible? It was to be stoned to death. Here we see the punishment of God for the blaspheming of His name, as hail rained down upon the people.

Revelation 16:21 says the weight of each hail was "a talent". The weight of a talent in scripture is 100 lbs. Imagine for a moment 100 lbs. hailstones raining down upon the earth. Where could they hide from the wrath of God? The mountains have crumbled and the cities have fallen. There was no way the people could protect themselves from the wrath of God. The people continued their blaspheme against God because of the plague of the hail, because the hailstones were so severe. This section ends like the preceding ones with a very vivid description of the terror of the final judgment.

16

THE DESTRUCTION OF THE ANTICHRIST KINGDOM

REVELATION 17:1-7 "THEN ONE OF THE SEVEN ANGELS who had the seven bowls came and spoke with me, saying, "Come here, I will show you the judgment of the great prostitute who sits on many waters, 2 with whom the kings of the earth committed acts of sexual immorality, and those who live on the earth became drunk with the wine of her sexual immorality." 3 And he carried me away in the Spirit into a wilderness; and I saw a woman sitting on a scarlet beast, full of blasphemous names, having seven heads and ten horns. 4 The woman was clothed in purple and scarlet, and adorned with gold, precious stones, and pearls, holding in her hand a gold cup full of abominations and of the unclean things of her sexual immorality, 5 and on her forehead a name was written, a mystery: "BABYLON THE GREAT, THE MOTHER OF PROSTITUTES AND OF THE ABOMINATIONS OF THE EARTH." 6 And I saw the woman drunk with the blood of the saints, and with the blood of the witnesses of Jesus. When I saw her, I wondered greatly. 7 And the angel said to me, "Why do you wonder? I will tell you the mystery of the woman and of the beast that carries her, which has the seven heads and the ten horns."

John stood amazed at the carnage that had taken place upon the earth. An angel who had poured his bowl upon the earth approached John and said to him, "Come here, I will show you the judgment of the great prostitute who sits on many waters, with whom the kings of the earth committed acts of sexual immorality, and those who live on the earth became drunk with the wine of her sexual immorality."

In the great city of Babylon, run by the Antichrist, John saw this city as a prostitute, one who sells her body for money. The woman was sitting on a seven-headed beast, which stands on water. We know from scripture that the water represents many people of different nationalities (Revelation 17:15), but who is this woman? Let us take a little closer look at her. This woman was dressed in purple and scarlet and was glittering with gold, precious stones, and pearls.

The city was described in purple and scarlet, which were colors of splendor and magnificence. The dyes used to make fabric these colors were rare and costly in John's time period. Purple and scarlet were the colors of rulers, whether economic or political. The colors were reserved for royalty or the church hierarchy. So, the colors indicate that the woman had power and influence. Obviously, the city was very wealthy through the prosperity of the Antichrist. Babylon is the descriptive name for the value system of the ungodly age and the kingdom of the Antichrist.

If you followed the Antichrist, he promised to give you all the splendors of the world, but for a price. The Antichrist would supply all the desires of your heart if you would only follow him. Sounds familiar doesn't it.

In Luke 4:1-13, Satan came to Jesus in the wilderness tempting Jesus in three areas that correspond to temptations common to all of us today: the lust of the flesh; the lust of the eyes or covetousness; and the pride of life, or lust for power. What Christ did through these temptations reveals a pattern for believers to follow. The temptation to sin or disobey God is a basic experience all people encounter. Jesus demonstrated the proper response to resist with the help of God and His Word, which is our most powerful weapon to refute the lies of the devil.

Satan and this world promise you all the sinful desires your heart could want, but only offers you eternal death in return.

On the woman's forehead was a name, "BABYLON THE GREAT, THE MOTHER OF PROSTITUTES AND OF THE ABOMINATIONS OF THE EARTH." In spite of all her glamour, she is nothing but a prostitute. One of the chief features of this city is her harlotry. When people give their hearts to idols and things that take the place of God, the Scriptures call it whoredom, adultery, and fornication.

We read that this harlot, or prostitute, is sitting on a strange-looking beast. He is a scarlet beast that was covered with blasphemous names and had seven heads and ten horns. This is the same beast (seven heads and ten horns) that was previously seen in Revelation 13:1. This Beast is the Antichrist and he ruled as a dictator over all of this city's wealth and pleasures, giving those who followed him the desires of their hearts.

This harlot is the seat of the godless civilization that leads people to sin. Notice that her influence is first with the kings or leaders and then with all the inhabitants of the earth. She is seated on the beast, the Antichrist from whom she gets her power and whom she leads men to worship. Her close relationship with the world meant that she has received riches and honors from mankind who dwelt upon the earth in the kingdom of the Antichrist. This city is a prostitute, who leads people away from God into idolatry She is intoxicated with the blood of the saints of God. The whole purpose of this great city, this dominion of power, the prosperity of her wealth was due to the power and authority of the Antichrist.

> Revelation 17:8-13 "The beast that you saw was, and is not, and is about to come up out of the abyss and go to destruction. And those who live on the earth, whose names have not been written in the book of life from the foundation of the world, will wonder when they see the beast, that he was, and is not, and will come. 9 Here is the mind which has wisdom. The seven heads are seven mountains upon which the woman sits, 10 and they are seven kings; five have fallen, one is, the other has not yet come; and when he comes, he must remain a little while. 11 The beast which was, and is not, is himself also an eighth and is one of the seven, and he goes to destruction, 12 The ten horns which you saw are ten kings who have not yet received a kingdom, but they receive authority as kings with the beast for one

hour. 13 These have one purpose, and they give their
power and authority to the beast."

The angels who had been describing the city now explained the
meaning of the beast and the prostitute to John.

The Antichrist, empowered by Satan, controls human society, using
his power to fight against the authority of God. Interpreting the vision
becomes more difficult when the angel gives further details of the
seven rulers. Most of them already belong to the past. Only one is yet
to appear, though he will be replaced by an eighth, who will display
even greater satanic power than the previous seven.

There will always be rulers and nations who will want to join
forces with the Antichrist. They see benefits for themselves in being
part of the ungodly power system. They give wholehearted support to
the Antichrist, but their apparent success is brief. It is only seven years
long. The ten horns you saw are ten kings who have not yet received
a kingdom, but who for one hour will receive authority as kings along
with the beast. The kings had one purpose, to give their power and
authority to the beast.

In our world today we have a United Nations Security Council made
up of five permanent members and ten non-permanent members. The
five permanent members are China, France, the Russian Federation, the
United Kingdom, and the United States. The functions and powers of
the Security Council are as follows; 1) to maintain international peace
and security in accordance with the principles and purposes of the
United Nations; 2) to investigate any dispute or situation which might
lead to international friction; 3) To recommend methods of adjusting

such disputes or the terms of settlement; 4) to formulate plans for the establishment of a system to regulate armaments; 5) to determine the existence of a threat to the peace or act of aggression and to recommend what action should be taken; 6) to call on Members to apply economic sanctions and other measures not involving the use of force to prevent or stop aggression; 7) and to take military action against an aggressor. (https://www.un.org/securitycouncil/content/functions-and-powers)

No, I am not saying that these world powers are the ones in the end times, but we have a political system that is set up the same way it will be during the time of the Antichrist and his power.

In the end times, the world divides into ten regions with ten leaders (10 horns, 10 crowns). The Antichrist will manifest himself throughout the earthly kingdoms and be the ultimate ruler over all the kings and their kingdoms.

> Revelation 17:15-18 "And he said to me, "The waters which you saw where the prostitute sits are peoples and multitudes, and nations and languages. 16 And the ten horns which you saw, and the beast, these will hate the prostitute and will make her desolate and naked, and will eat her flesh and will burn her up with fire. 17 For God has put it in their hearts to execute His purpose by having a common purpose, and by giving their kingdom to the beast, until the words of God will be fulfilled. 18 The woman whom you saw is the great city, which reigns over the kings of the earth."

In their pursuit of power and prosperity, people may develop international cooperation, but hatred and jealousy eventually bring disunity and conflict. This city has relied on the Antichrist to give her power and it is now destroyed. The beast that supported her has now left her empty and desolate.

That is what sin does. It may seem to fill a void in your life, but then you are left empty and still alone, seeking to fill that emptiness in your life. It is no different than what we see here in the city of Babylon.

The Antichrist promised so much for the people who followed him, but they are left empty, tortured, and soon would find eternal death.

Sin is deceptive in nature. The writer of Hebrews warned against being "hardened through the deceitfulness of sin" (Hebrews 3:13). Sin misleads you. It looks very appealing, but its true nature is disguised. The devil loves to sugarcoat sin to make it as appealing as possible. There is no doubt that there is pleasure in sin, but in the end, it leaves you empty.

The Bible calls sin the "passing pleasure" (Hebrews 11:25). Sin offers temporary pleasure at the price of long-term pain. The goal of sin is to make you, its slave.

> John 8:34-36 "Jesus answered them, "Truly, truly I say to you, everyone who commits sin is a slave of sin. 35 Now the slave does not remain in the house forever; the son does remain forever. 36 So if the Son sets you free, you really will be free."

The problem with sin is that it is never satisfied. It always asks for more. Once you indulge in a form of lust, you will be drawn to it more and more. Like a drug addiction, it keeps drawing you further and further into its chains.

> Revelation 18:1-8 "After these things I saw another angel coming down from heaven, having great authority, and the earth was illuminated from his glory. 2 And he cried out with a mighty voice, saying, "Fallen, fallen is Babylon the great! She has become a dwelling place of demons and a prison of every unclean spirit, and a prison of every unclean and hateful bird. 3 For all the nations have fallen because of the wine of the passion of her sexual immorality, and the kings of the earth have committed acts of sexual immorality with her, and the merchants of the earth have become rich from the excessive wealth of her luxury. 4 I heard another voice from heaven, saying, "Come out of her, my people, so that you will not participate in her sins and receive any of her plagues; 5 for her sins have piled up as high as heaven, and God has remembered her offenses. 6 Pay her back even as she has paid, and give back to her double according to her deeds; in the cup which she has mixed, mix twice as much for her. 7 To the extent that she glorified herself and lived luxuriously, to the same extent give her torment and mourning; for she says in her heart, 'I sit as a queen and I am not a widow,

and will never see mourning.' 8 For this reason in one day her plagues will come, plague and mourning and famine, and she will be burned up with fire; for the Lord God who judges her is strong."

Notice the depravity of the city. This depravity includes the sin of godlessness. This system of the Antichrist is actually infested with demon worship. The system of the Antichrist and the system of Babylon is a system of Satanism. God has said that this is fornication.

Fornication is used in the Bible in two major ways. First, it means the actual, physical sin of sexual immorality. Secondly, it means the sin of unfaithfulness and spiritual immorality, lusting after other gods and worshipping other gods. Here in Revelation, it is the worship of the Antichrist.

Babylon will succumb to sudden and total destruction. All that will be left are the demons and vultures to haunt her dwelling, devouring the men and women who dwelled there. Despite the boast of her lavished prosperity, God will judge her and burn the empire down. The destruction will be so quick and unexpected, that in a single day it will be destroyed. One day she is boasting about her wealth. The very next day she is burning. "For this reason in one day her plagues will come, plague and mourning and famine, and she will be burned up with fire; for the Lord God who judges her is strong."

Revelation 18:9–10 "And the kings of the earth, who committed acts of sexual immorality and lived luxuriously with her, will weep and mourn over her when they see the smoke of her burning, 10 standing at a distance because of the fear of her torment, saying, 'Woe, woe, the great city, Babylon, the strong city! For in one hour your judgment has come.'

In this great judgment of the final overthrow of Babylon the great was briefly mentioned. Both Revelation 17 and Revelation 18 are telling of that same event. Revelation 18 shows us Babylon's final overthrow during the last judgment.

Revelation 18:11-20 "And the merchants of the earth weep and mourn over her, because no one buys their cargo any more 12 cargo of gold, silver, precious stones, and pearls; fine linen, purple, silk, and scarlet; every kind of citron wood, every article of ivory, and every article made from very valuable wood, bronze, iron, and marble; 13 cinnamon, spice, incense, perfume, frankincense, wine, olive oil, fine flour, wheat, cattle, sheep, and cargo of horses, carriages, slaves, and human lives. 14 The fruit you long for has left you, and all things that were luxurious and splendid have passed away from you and people will no longer find them. 15 The merchants of these things, who became rich from her, will stand at a distance because of the fear of her torment, weeping and mourning, 16 saying, 'Woe, woe, the great city, she who was clothed in fine linen and purple and scarlet, and adorned with gold, precious stones, and pearls; 17 for in one hour such great wealth has been laid waste!' And every shipmaster and every passenger and sailor, and all who make their living by the sea, stood at a distance, 18 and were crying out as they saw the smoke of her burning, saying, 'What city is like the great city?' 19 And they threw dust on their heads and were crying out, weeping and mourning, saying, 'Woe, woe, the great city, in which all who had ships at sea became rich from her prosperity, for in one hour she has been laid waste!' 20 Rejoice over her, O heaven, and you saints and apostles and prophets, because God has pronounced judgment for you against her."

What were these people who were in such torment, grieved about? The loss of their things, their pleasures, their treasures. Everything that they found value in has now been destroyed. That is what happens to those who make money and power their god, as Babylon did. Quickly and unexpectedly, at a time when they least expect it, their entire empire will come crashing down.

Anything that seduces and entices God's people to rebel against Him, whether it be doctrines, theologies, religions, or anything that takes you from faithfulness to God, is a spiritual prostitute. These merchants, buyers, and sellers grew rich in this kingdom of the beast. There were excessive luxuries that enticed and seduced many people. Their absolute power in this kingdom was brought through the deception of the Antichrist.

2 Corinthians 4:3-4 "And even if our gospel is veiled, it is veiled to those who are perishing, 4in whose case the god of this world has blinded the minds of the unbelieving so that they will not see the light of the gospel of the glory of Christ, who is the image of God."

How easy was it for the Antichrist to seduce the people? It was easy. All he had to do was cater to their wants and desires. The promise of prosperity appealed to the heart's desires of the people. All these "things" will become worthless on the day of the Lord's wrath. We do not need to envy wicked men in all their success and riches. It is their portion, and without Christ, it is all they are ever going to have.

Remember, we are approaching the time when the earth will be destroyed, but we do not know when or how long God will delay His wrath. When God begins to enter into judgment with His enemies, the strongest arm of flesh cannot prevail, and kings with their armies will flee, the stoutest hearts will be afraid and terrified. God will always prevail. No matter what Satan may try, God will always be victorious.

Revelation 18:21-24 "Then a strong angel picked up a stone like a great millstone and threw it into the sea, saying, "So will Babylon, the great city, be thrown down with violence, and will never be found again. 22 And the sound of harpists, musicians, flute players, and trumpeters will never be heard in you again; and no craftsman of any craft will ever be found in you again; and the sound of a mill will never be heard in you again; 23 and the light of a lamp will never shine in you again; and the voice of the groom and bride will never be heard in you again; for your merchants were the powerful people of the earth, because all the nations were deceived by your witchcraft. 24 And in her was found the blood of prophets and of saints, and of all who have been slaughtered on the earth."

John watched in amazement as suddenly a great angel picked up a huge stone, that resembled a millstone and hurled it to the sea. The waves crested over the great city leaving it in ruin. At that moment, the destruction of the city reminded John of another great city that was destroyed within an hour of its destruction, the city of Sodom and Gomorrah.

Genesis 19: 24-29 "Then the Lord rained brimstone and fire on Sodom and Gomorrah from the Lord out of heaven, 25 and He overthrew those cities, and all the surrounding area, and all the inhabitants of the cities, and what grew on the ground. 26 But Lot's wife, from behind him, looked back, and she became a pillar of salt.27 Now Abraham got up early in the morning and went to the place where he had stood before the Lord; 28 and he looked down toward Sodom and Gomorrah, and toward all the land of the surrounding area; and behold, he saw the smoke of the land ascended like the smoke of a furnace.29 So it came about, when God destroyed the cities of the surrounding area, that God remembered Abraham, and sent Lot out of the midst of the destruction, when He overthrew the cities in which Lot had lived."

Just as quick and terrible was God's wrath upon the cities of Sodom and Gomorrah, so was the wrath on the city of the Antichrist. In an instant, the city fell silent. All that was left was the burning embers of a once-great city, that are now laid in ruins.

Revelation 19:1-6 "After these things I heard something like a loud voice of a great multitude in heaven, saying, "Hallelujah! Salvation, glory, and power belong to our God, 2 because His judgments are true and righteous; for He has judged the great prostitute who was corrupting the earth with her sexual immorality, and He has avenged the blood of His bond-servants on her." 3 And a second time they said, "Hallelujah! Her smoke rises forever and ever." 4 And the twenty-four elders and the four living creatures fell down and worshiped God who sits on the throne, saying, "Amen. Hallelujah!" 5 And a voice came from the throne, saying, "Give praise to our God, all you His bond-servants, you who fear Him, the small and the great." 6 "Then I heard something like the voice of a great multitude and like the sound of many waters, and like the sound of mighty peals of thunder, saying, "Hallelujah! For the Lord our God, the Almighty, reigns."

John's ears filled with a cheer and the sound of celebration in Heaven to God. The multitude of voices surrounded him in the presence of his Savior. Again, the praise and worship resounded in celebration of God for His works and the overwhelming judgment of His victory. "Give praise to our God, all you His bond-servants, you who fear Him, the small and the great." "Hallelujah! For the Lord our God, the Almighty, reigns."

THE WEDDING FEAST OF THE LAMB

Revelation 19:7-10 "Let's rejoice and be glad and give the glory to Him, because the marriage of the Lamb has come, and His bride has prepared herself." 8 It was given to her to clothe herself in fine linen, bright and clean; for the fine linen is the righteous acts of the saints. 9 Then he said to me, "Write: 'Blessed are those who are invited to the wedding feast of the Lamb.'" And he said to me, "These are the true words of God." 10 Then I fell at his feet to worship him. But he said to me, "Do not do that; I am a fellow servant of yours and your brothers and sisters who hold the testimony of Jesus; worship God! For the testimony of Jesus is the spirit of prophecy."

There before the throne in heaven was a great table as far as the eye could see, ordained with decorations and filled with every type of food. This table was prepared for a great feast. The angel told John that this is a wedding feast. "Blessed are those who are invited to the wedding feast of the Lamb." At that moment John understood that the time of celebration had come for the body of Christ was with her groom at the house of the Father.

The most anticipated day in the life of every believer is the day that they will be with the Lord forever. It is the day on which the final consummation comes with our Lord. Make no mistake, the church has but one desire, one treasure, and one anticipation, and that is Christ.

> Philippians 3:7-8 "But whatever things were gain to me, these things I have counted as loss because of Christ. 8 More than that, I count all things to be loss in view of the surpassing value of knowing Christ Jesus my Lord, for whom I have suffered the loss of all things, and count them mere rubbish, so that I may gain Christ"

In a wedding ceremony, the groom and the bride come together to make vows to each other celebrating the life they will spend together. After the ceremony, the couple would have a reception together to celebrate with their family and friends the union of their life together as man and wife. After the reception, the groom takes his bride home to a place that he has prepared for her, to spend their life together.

So is the image of what occurs between Jesus, the Groom, and His Church, the bride. Throughout the New Testament, there are pieces of this type of wedding imagery used to describe the relationship between Jesus Christ and His Church. If you are a member of His body, which is the Church, you are part of the description of this wedding ceremony and the wedding feast of the Lamb. In a sense, you married Christ when you promised to love, honor, cherish, and obey only Him.

In Revelation 21:2 we see a comparison with Revelation 19:7 "I saw the Holy City, The New Jerusalem, coming down out of heaven from God, prepared as a bride beautifully dressed for her husband."

In Revelation 19:7 we see it says: "Let's rejoice and be glad and give the glory to Him, because the marriage of the Lamb has come, and His bride has prepared herself." 8 It was given to her to clothe herself in fine linen, bright and clean; for the fine linen is the righteous acts of the saints."

John used the analogy of a bridegroom and bride to show the preeminence of the Lord. In John 3:26-30 Jesus is shown as the Bridegroom. In his letter to the believers in Ephesians 5:32, Paul equates Christian marriage to the union that exists spiritually between Christ and His bride, the Church. In Revelation 19:7-8 we see the preparation of the bride through the work of the Groom.

"Let's rejoice and be glad and give the glory to Him, because the marriage of the Lamb has come, and His bride has prepared herself. It was given to her to clothe herself in fine linen, bright and clean; for the fine linen is the righteous acts of the saints." It was through the gift of the groom that we are prepared for Him. The fine linen of the bride has been made white by the blood of the Lamb. This "righteousness" was not ours until we received the Lord Jesus into our lives and took on

His righteousness. Our own righteousness had been as filthy rags, but Jesus replaced the filth with His righteousness. The bride's clothes are clean and bright representing her sinlessness before God, having been washed in the blood of the Lamb.

In Bible times, Jewish custom required the groom to go to the bride's father to establish a price for marrying his daughter, this was called a dowry. It same is true for us in our marriage covenant with Jesus. Jesus as our Groom has paid the price for our lives with His own blood. The more we understand God's idea of marriage, the more we understand Heaven and His commitment to us. God's covenant is an invitation to enter into a relationship in which He promises: "I will be your God and you will be My people" (Exodus 19:5).

A covenant is a commitment that God initiates and upholds. The whole marital covenant is characterized by love. If we view love as mere attraction plus emotion, we have a shallow view of both love and marriage. God's demonstration of love is an unconditional, sacrificial, mature, compassionate, and eternal commitment.

Our price has been paid. We have taken our vows by accepting Jesus as our Savior, and one day we will stand before the Father in an eternal celebration of being home, with a lifetime of love that we get to share in as we are finally forever with our Groom.

17

THE FINAL BATTLE

REVELATION 19:11-19 "AND I SAW HEAVEN OPENED, AND behold, a white horse, and He who sat on it is called Faithful and True, and in righteousness He judges and wages war. 12 His eyes are a flame of fire, and on His head are many crowns; and He has a name written on Him which no one knows except Himself. 13 He is clothed with a robe dipped in blood, and His name is called The Word of God. 14 And the armies which are in heaven, clothed in fine linen, white and clean, were following Him on white horses. 15 From His mouth comes a sharp sword, so that with it He may strike down the nations, and He will rule them with a rod of iron; and He treads the wine press of the fierce wrath of God, the Almighty. 16 And on His robe and on His thigh He has a name written: "KING OF KINGS, AND LORD OF LORDS."17 Then I saw an angel standing in the sun, and he cried out with a loud voice, saying to all the birds that fly in midheaven, "Come, assemble for the great feast of God, 18 so that you may eat the flesh of kings and the flesh of commanders, the flesh of mighty men, the flesh of horses and of those who sit on them, and the flesh of all people, both free and slaves, and

small and great." 19 And I saw the beast and the kings of
the earth and their armies, assembled to make war against
Him who sat on the horse, and against His army."

As John stood up from his worship, the heavens seemed to split open
and there was Jesus, majestically sitting on a white horse. His eyes were
intense and on His head were many crowns. His robe looked as if it had
been dipped in blood and His name was shouted in victory as He is the
Word of God. Behind Jesus stood a vast army that was far too many to
count, following on white horses of their own. The army that follow
Christ was the Church, following their leader into battle.

From his mouth He brought forth the Word of God, as a sharp
double-edged sword, which tore through the armies that had gathered
together for the final battle of Armageddon.

In an instant, Jesus snatched the Antichrist and the False Prophet, who
deceived the world and cast them alive into the Lake of Fire, which burns
with brimstone. The rest of mankind, who wore the mark of the beast,
were slaughtered by the Word of Jesus. There was no need for battle, only
a single word of Jesus. The kings and men of the earth who followed the
Antichrist were struck down with a single blow. Then an announcement
of the angel rung down upon the earth. The angel said, "All the birds of
the air, still left upon the earth, to come feast upon the bodies of the men
who defied Christ." He said, "Come, assemble for the great feast of God,
so that you may eat the flesh of kings and the flesh of commanders, the
flesh of mighty men, the flesh of horses and of those who sit on them,
and the flesh of all people, both free and slaves, and small and great." All
the birds were filled with their flesh. The battle was over. Not a single

follower of the Antichrist was left. The bodies of the kings and of men were left scattered all throughout the valley of Megiddo, filling it with blood up to a horse's bridle. The battle was over. The victory was won.

> Revelation 20:1-3 "Then I saw an angel coming down from heaven, holding the key of the abyss and a great chain in his hand. 2 And he took hold of the dragon, the serpent of old, who is the devil and Satan, and bound him for a thousand years; 3 and he threw him into the abyss and shut it and sealed it over him, so that he would not deceive the nations any longer, until the thousand years were completed; after these things he must be released for a short time."

Satan stood off in a distance watching the destruction of his empire that he had made, now come to an end. A sudden flush of anger raged through Satan as he watched the destruction of his kingdom that he had built. Furious words rang from his lips as he cursed God in rage. In his anger, he failed to notice the mighty angel who had swooped down from heaven holding the key to the abyss. The angel grabbed Satan from where he stood, wrapping him with a mighty chain, and then began to drag him into the depths of the abyss. Satan who was now chained in the depths of the mighty pit of the abyss, watched as the door was shut and sealed over him, where he was left alone in his torment for one thousand years. For a thousand years, Satan was bound. No longer could he cause destruction. No longer could he cause pain and temptation. The world was free from his deception.

18

THE MILLENNIAL KINGDOM

Revelation 20:4-6 "Then I saw thrones, and they sat on them, and judgment was given to them. And I saw the souls of those who had been beheaded because of their testimony of Jesus and because of the word of God, and those who had not worshiped the beast or his image, and had not received the mark on their foreheads and on their hands; and they came to life and reigned with Christ for a thousand years. 5 The rest of the dead did not come to life until the thousand years were completed. This is the first resurrection. 6 Blessed and holy is the one who has a part in the first resurrection; over these the second death has no power, but they will be priests of God and of Christ, and will reign with Him for a thousand years."

In a world that is desperate for peace, the Millennial Reign of Jesus Christ will be a welcomed time of peace for all of mankind. The Millennial Reign will be a period of time in which Jesus Christ will reign on Earth for 1,000 years as the sovereign ruler in the fulfillment of many Old and New Testament prophecies. Satan, who is now bound in the bottomless pit will have no influence on the earth to deceive mankind. Jesus' rule will span the entire world. He will be King of Kings and Lord of Lords upon this Earth. He will also sit on the throne of His father, David, ruling over Israel. Israel will be re-gathered from the nations and restored to the land under the rule of the Messiah, Jesus Christ. The prophet Isaiah also wrote of the coming kingdom of Jesus Christ.

> Isaiah 9:6-7 "For a Child will be born to us, a Son will be given to us; And the government will rest on His shoulders; And His name will be called Wonderful Counselor, Mighty God, Eternal Father, Prince of Peace. 7 There will be no end to the increase of His government or of peace On the throne of David and over his kingdom, To establish it and to uphold it with justice and righteousness From then on and forevermore. The zeal of the Lord of armies will accomplish this."

Isaiah stated that the governments would be on His shoulders, signifying that He would have full responsibility for ruling all the world. He declared that Jesus would be called Wonderful Counselor, and the Mighty God, and the Everlasting Father, affirming His eternal existence. Isaiah refers to Him as the Prince of Peace, declaring Him as the true peacemaker; the one coming to bring peace to the entire world. And finally, Jesus will sit on the throne of David ordering and establishing it with judgment and justice. This will be a pure theocracy, a system of government in which Christ will be completely in charge. Jesus will personally and visibly rule from the Holy City, Jerusalem.

He will establish a perfectly righteous rule over the entire earth. He will execute perfect justice in every case. The city that once received so much persecution and unrest will be the very center of joy, comfort, and peace.

> Micah 4:2–4 "Many nations will come and say, "Come and let's go up to the mountain of the Lord And to the house of the God of Jacob, So that He may teach us about His ways, And that we may walk in His paths." For from Zion will go forth the law, And the word of the Lord from Jerusalem. 3 And He will judge between many peoples And render decisions for mighty, distant nations. Then they will beat their swords into plowshares, And their spears into pruning hooks; Nation will not lift a sword against nation, And never again will they train for war. 4 Instead, each of them will sit under his vine And under his fig tree, With no one to make them afraid, Because the mouth of the Lord of armies has spoken."

What will the earth be like during this millennial period? The earth that was once devested by sin will be made new again. I believe that after all that has taken place during the tribulation period, the earth will be restored to its natural beauty. The animals will not fear humans and the humans will be at peace with the animals. We will live in peace as it was before the flood of Noah, before God placed fear in the hearts of the animals.

> Genesis 9:2-3 "The fear of you and the terror of you
> will be on every animal of the earth and on every bird
> of the sky; on everything that crawls on the ground,
> and on all the fish of the sea. They are handed over to
> you. 3 Every moving thing that is alive shall be food
> for you; I have given everything to you, as I gave the
> green plant."

Up until the time of the flood of Noah, every animal and human was a vegetarian. That is why there is no problem for every kind of animal to be on the ark together. They did not desire flesh and blood.

And once again during this time, we see that there will be no fear in the hearts of mankind.

> Isaiah 11:6-10 "And the wolf will dwell with the lamb,
> And the leopard will lie down with the young goat,
> And the calf and the young lion and the fattened steer
> will be together; And a little boy will lead them. 7Also
> the cow and the bear will graze, Their young will lie
> down together, And the lion will eat straw like the ox.
> 8The nursing child will play by the hole of the cobra,
> And the weaned child will put his hand on the viper's
> den. 9They will not hurt or destroy in all My holy
> mountain, For the earth will be full of the knowledge
> of the LORD As the waters cover the sea. 10Then on
> that day The nations will resort to the root of Jesse,

Who will stand as a signal flag for the peoples; And His resting place will be glorious."

During this thousand-year period of time on earth, there will be believers who have died before the rapture, those who have been raptured, and the martyrs who died during the tribulation. All of these people have their new glorified bodies. Also, on this earth are those who accepted Christ as their Savior during the tribulation period, not killed at the battle of Armageddon. These people who made it through the tribulation period and have trusted Christ as their Savior will still have their sinful bodies. Those who are still on earth with their original sinful bodies will still have a day that they will die. But at this time on earth, mankind will have the longevity that it once did before the flood when mankind lived up to 900 years of age.

> Isaiah 65:17–25 "For behold, I create new heavens and a new earth; And the former things will not be remembered or come to mind.18 "But be glad and rejoice forever in what I create; For behold, I create Jerusalem for rejoicing And her people for gladness. 19 "I will also rejoice in Jerusalem and be glad in My people; And there will no longer be heard in her The voice of weeping and the sound of crying. 20 "No longer will there be in it an infant who lives but a few days, Or an old man who does not live out his days; For the youth will die at the age of one hundred And the one who does not reach the age of one hundred

Will be thought accursed. 21 "They will build houses and inhabit them; They will also plant vineyards and eat their fruit. 22 "They will not build and another inhabit, They will not plant and another eat; For as the lifetime of a tree, so will be the days of My people, And My chosen ones will wear out the work of their hands. 23 "They will not labor in vain, Or bear children for calamity; For they are the offspring of those blessed by the Lord, And their descendants with them. 24 It will also come to pass that before they call, I will answer; and while they are still speaking, I will hear. 25 The wolf and the lamb will graze together, and the lion will eat straw like the ox; and dust will be the serpent's food. They will do no evil or harm in all My holy mountain," says the Lord."

Another major revelation is given in Psalm 72, revealing Christ's reign over the whole earth. After describing how He will judge the people, defend the afflicted, and deliver the righteous, Psalm 72 concludes by stating that all nations will be blessed through Him and that the whole earth will be filled with His glory. This is the expectation of what the millennial kingdom will be like. A time of peace, but only for a limited time.

19

The End

At the end of the thousand-year period of time on this earth, Satan will be loosed for a short period. Up unto the end of the thousand years, God prevents Satan from deceiving and influencing humanity.

> Revelation 20:7-10 "When the thousand years are completed, Satan will be released from his prison, 8 and will come out to deceive the nations which are at the four corners of the earth, Gog and Magog, to gather them together for the war; the number of them is like the sand of the seashore. 9 And they came up on the broad plain of the earth and surrounded the camp of the saints and the beloved city, and fire came down from heaven and devoured them. 10 And the devil who deceived them was thrown into the lake of fire and brimstone, where the beast and the false prophet are also; and they will be tormented day and night forever and ever."

After a thousand years, God will release Satan from the bottomless pit and he will be allowed to deceive the nations one last time. After Satan's release, he once again will deceive mankind to turn people against

God one more time. This just goes to show man's depravity. We are not as civil as we would like to believe. Given the right circumstances, mankind is a breath away from civil anarchy. The millennium will prove the depth of man's rebellion and wickedness. This time period will confirm that man's innate depravity exists. At the close of the thousand years, Satan will be released and gather these defiant ones in yet another worldwide rebellion against God. Where do all of these people come from that come up against God after Satan is loosed? These are descendants of those who made it through the tribulation period. For a thousand years, those who still had their sinful bodies had the ability to populate the earth.

Those who will come against God will have walked with Jesus Christ, talked with Jesus Christ, and lived with Him for a thousand years under his reign.

When Satan is loosed, he will go right back to his old ways of temptation and deception. He actually is able to convince people that Jesus Christ was lying, that He is not the true God and that Jesus was only deceiving them and people will believe it. He will find many who are only too willing to listen to his lies. They will rejoice at his bold claims, flock to his standards, and follow him headlong into a rebellion. The insurrection will spread like a prairie fire fanned by a high wind, but this rebellion will not succeed. This rebellion is only permitted by God in order to bring to light the hidden works of darkness of the human heart. The people who have gathered together against Jesus Chris will be stuck down in a blaze of fire from heaven. John says "and fire came down from God out of heaven, and devoured them." The judgment is swift and sure. With a flash, the fire of God falls and it is all over. Nothing remains but a heap of ashes. No birds are summoned and there was no reason to bury these dead. They are cremated in the fires that slay them. Only Satan will be left and God is about to deal with him.

> Revelation 20:10 "And the devil who deceived them was thrown into the lake of fire and brimstone, where the beast and the false prophet are also; and they will be tormented day and night forever and ever."

At this time Satan will be cast into the Lake of Fire to suffer forever. Satan's punishment will be the same as all those who refused to accept the gift of salvation through Jesus Christ, an eternity in Hell. Satan will be with all those he has led astray, burning, suffering, and tortured forever in the burning flames and sulfurs of the Lake of Fire.

Satan's judgment was ensured at the cross, but the actual execution of the sentence awaits the end of the millennium and his last rebellion.

Hell was prepared as the place prepared for Satan and those angels who followed him. The one who has brought untold sorrow and suffering to all mankind must now suffer for all eternity without relief.

> Matthew 25:41 "Then He will also say to those on His left, 'Depart from Me, you accursed people, into the eternal fire which has been prepared for the devil and his angels;"

2 Peter 2:4 "For if God did not spare angels when they sinned, but cast them into hell and committed them to pits of darkness, held for judgment;"

Maurice Rawlings, a cardiologist, and professor of medicine at the University of Tennessee College of Medicine was also a devout atheist. But in 1977, while trying to resuscitate a man who had been screaming in terror, something happened that changed his thinking. He gave this report to Omni Magazine.

"Each time he regained heartbeat and respiration the patient screamed, "I am in hell." He was terrified and pleading with me to help him. I was scared to death. Then I noticed a real alarmed look on his face. He had a terrified look worse than the expression seen in death. This patient had a grotesque grimace expression of sheer horror. His pupils were dilated and he was perspiring and trembling. He looked as if his hair was on end! Then still another strange thing happened. He said "Don't you understand? I am in hell. Don't let me go back to hell. The man was serious and it finally occurred to me that he was indeed in trouble.

He was in a panic like I had never seen before. Dr. Rawlings said "No one, who could have heard his screams and saw the look of terror on his face could doubt for a single minute that he was actually in a place called hell." ("To Hell and Back, Book by Maurice Rawlings chapters. indigo.ca". www.chapters.indigo.ca. Published: September 6, 1993")

Hell is a place that was originally created for the devil and his angels. Because of man's sin and refusal to accept Jesus as their Savior,

The Beginning of the End

it will be their place of punishment forever. Hell, and the Lake of Fire are described as a place of eternal separation from God, eternal death, torment, shame, and misery, weeping and gnashing of teeth, and the death of both body and soul. The Bible calls Hell an eternal fire, an unquenchable fire where the worm does not die, the Lake of Fire, and brimstone. Hell will be unending torture and a place of everlasting punishment. (Matthew 8:12, Matthew 13:42, Matthew 25:46, Mark 9:44, Luke 16:23-24, Jude 13, Revelation 14:11, Revelation 20:15)

The worst part is those who will be in Hell and the Lake of Fire is that they will be separated from God forever. This place is reserved for everyone who refuses to accept the gift of salvation through Jesus Christ and the forgiveness of their sins.

THE GREAT WHITE THRONE JUDGEMENT

> Revelation 20:11-15 "Then I saw a great white throne and Him who sat upon it, from whose presence earth and heaven fled, and no place was found for them. 12 And I saw the dead, the great and the small, standing before the throne, and books were opened; and another book was opened, which is the book of life; and the dead were judged from the things which were written in the books, according to their deeds. 13 And the sea gave up the dead who were in it, and Death and Hades gave up the dead who were in them; and they were judged, each one of them according to their deeds. 14

Then Death and Hades were thrown into the lake of fire. This is the second death, the lake of fire. 15 And if anyone's name was not found written in the book of life, he was thrown into the lake of fire."

John looked upon the sea of people who now stood before the throne of God. There stood people who were tormented, burnt, and screaming in fear as they stood before the throne in heaven. John watched as Jesus approached the throne having two books. As Jesus opened the first book not a single name of anyone, who stood before the Great White Throne, had been written in the book. Jesus closed the book and set it aside. He took the next book, opened it, and one by one He judged the people who stood before the throne as they pleaded and cried in a loud voice for mercy, as their tears rolled down their face and the pain of anguish was upon their body. There was no mercy for them. One by one they were taken screaming to the lake of fire. As the people watched, screams seemed to fill Heaven as the wails of the people cried in horror as they were taken away to everlasting suffering.

The final judgment is coming. That day when all unbelievers will stand before God and give an account to God. The final judgment is called the "Great White Throne Judgment". The Great White Throne Judgment does not determine salvation. Everyone at the Great White Throne is an unbeliever who has rejected Christ in life and is therefore already doomed to the Lake of Fire.

The great judgment day ought not to frighten the Christian. Our sin is blotted out. Our sin is washed away. Our sin is deleted when we repent of it. The judgment day for the Christian will be a day of rejoicing. We will have our own judgment seat, but it is not like the judgment seat at the Great White Throne. The Christian judgment seat is a reward ceremony for believers for the victory through Christ. There will be no judgment of our sins because they have been forgiven, washed away by the blood of Christ when He died on the cross for us.

For those who stand before the Great White Throne of God, they have rejected the great salvation of God's Son. They have rejected the only way to God.

Every unbeliever on the face of the earth will stand before God and be judged. In verse 12, we see the basis of judgment. There are two kinds of books kept in heaven. Both will be present at the Great White Throne judgment. There is the Lamb's Book of Life. This is the book where every human being who has accepted Jesus as their Savior, will have their names written in this book. The other book is the Book of Records. This book is the record of all the works of unbelievers. When a person's name is not found in the Lamb's Book of Life, then the Book of Records is opened, and he is judged out of them. The Book of Records shows the degree of punishment a person is to receive. Yes, that means a man such as Hitler will be punished more and judged much more severely than a petty thief. Both are doomed for Hell, but both will not suffer the same amount of punishment.

> John 12:48 "The one who rejects Me and does not
> accept My teachings has one who judges him: the word
> which I spoke. That will judge him on the last day."

There is the record of secret sins, sins committed in the dark and behind closed doors, of ill feelings within the heart, or even the evil thoughts of the mind. He will be judged and punished for exactly what he has done, no more and no less. No amount of good works and the keeping of God's laws can be sufficient enough to forgive sin. All their thoughts, words, and actions will be judged against God's perfect standard. There will be no reward for them, only eternal condemnation and punishment. The ones who die without Christ are judged and then separated from God forever.

> Revelation 20:14 "Then Death and Hades were thrown into the lake of fire. This is the second death, the lake of fire. 15 And if anyone's name was not found written in the book of life, he was thrown into the lake of fire."

20

THE NEW HEAVENS AND THE NEW EARTH

REVELATION 21:1-9 "THEN I SAW A NEW HEAVEN AND a new earth; for the first heaven and the first earth passed away, and there is no longer any sea. 2 And I saw the holy city, new Jerusalem, coming down out of heaven from God, prepared as a bride adorned for her husband. 3 And I heard a loud voice from the throne, saying, "Behold, the tabernacle of God is among the people, and He will dwell among them, and they shall be His people, and God Himself will be among them, 4 and He will wipe away every tear from their eyes; and there will no longer be any death; there will no longer be any mourning, or crying, or pain; the first things have passed away." 5 And He who sits on the throne said, "Behold, I am making all things new." And He said, "Write, for these words are faithful and true." 6 Then He said to me, "It is done. I am the Alpha and the Omega, the beginning and the end. I will give water to the one who thirsts from the spring of the water of life, without cost. 7 The one who overcomes will inherit these things, and I will be his God and he will be My son. 8 But for the cowardly, and unbelieving, and abominable, and murderers, and sexually immoral persons, and sorcerers, and idolaters, and all liars, their part will be in the lake that burns with fire and brimstone, which is the second death." 9 Then one of the seven angels who had the seven bowls, full of the seven last plagues, came and spoke with me, saying, "Come here, I will show you the bride, the wife of the Lamb."

This was a different scene that he just watched before the Great White Throne. The books had been shut and now Jesus stood at the altar as the praise and worship surrounded His name in celebration of the King, the Savior, the one true God.

As Jesus raised His hands, John watched the whole Earth crumble and disappear. The heavens became black like darkness as the whole universe had now become a blank slate. Then before John's eyes, he saw the universe created from out of nothing, as God formed a new universe full of planets and stars which seemed to sing the praises of God. It was nothing that John had ever seen before. The beauty and majesty of the universe left him speechless. The holy city of Jerusalem came down from heaven, beautifully adorned in precious jewels as a bride who was prepared for the wedding. A loud voice cried, "Behold, the tabernacle of God is among the people, and He will dwell among them, and they shall be His people, and God Himself will be among them, and He will wipe away every tear from their eyes; and there will no longer be any death; there will no longer be any mourning, or crying, or pain; the first things have passed away."

No more pain, no more tears, no more sin and suffering, just the perfect peace and everlasting joy and fulfillment in Jesus Christ. This joy overfilled John's heart with a passion he had never experienced before. Joy sprang from his lips as the praises from his mouth celebrated Jesus. Jesus stood and said with a loud voice, "Behold, I am making all things new." As he looked at John he said, "Write, for these words are faithful and true." John grabbed his scroll and paper and begin to write, "It is done. I am the Alpha and the Omega, the beginning and the end. I will give water to the one who thirsts from the spring of the water of life, without cost. The one who overcomes will inherit these things, and I will be his God and he will be My son. But for the cowardly, and unbelieving, and abominable, and murderers, and sexually immoral persons, and sorcerers, and idolaters, and all liars, their part will be in the lake that burns with fire and brimstone, which is the second death."

John quickly and precisely began to write every word of Jesus. Without missing a beat, John seemed to be filled with every perfect emotion that he had never experienced before. The passion, the joy, the life that he experienced was indescribable.

> Revelation 21:10-27 "And he carried me away in the Spirit to a great and high mountain, and showed me the holy city, Jerusalem, coming down out of heaven from God, 11 having the glory of God. Her brilliance was like a very valuable stone, like a stone of crystal-clear

jasper. 12 It had a great and high wall, with twelve gates, and at the gates twelve angels; and names were written on the gates, which are the names of the twelve tribes of the sons of Israel. 13 There were three gates on the east, three gates on the north, three gates on the south, and three gates on the west. 14 And the wall of the city had twelve foundation stones, and on them were the twelve names of the twelve apostles of the Lamb.15 The one who spoke with me had a gold measuring rod to measure the city, its gates, and its wall. 16 The city is laid out as a square, and its length is as great as the width; and he measured the city with the rod, twelve thousand stadia; its length, width, and height are equal. 17 And he measured its wall, 144 cubits, by human measurements, which are also angelic measurements. 18 The material of the wall was jasper; and the city was pure gold, like clear glass. 19 The foundation stones of the city wall were decorated with every kind of precious stone. The first foundation stone was jasper; the second, sapphire; the third, chalcedony; the fourth, emerald; 20 the fifth, sardonyx; the sixth, sardius; the seventh, chrysolite; the eighth, beryl; the ninth, topaz; the tenth, chrysoprase; the eleventh, jacinth; the twelfth, amethyst. 21 And the twelve gates were twelve pearls; each one of the gates was a single pearl. And the street of the city was pure gold, like transparent glass."

22 "I saw no temple in it, for the Lord God the Almighty and the Lamb are its temple. 23 And the city has no need of the sun or of the moon to shine on it, for the glory of God has illuminated it, and its lamp is the Lamb. 24 The nations will walk by its light, and the kings of the earth will bring their glory into it. 25 In the daytime (for there will be no night there) its gates will never be closed; 26 and they will bring the glory and the honor of the nations into it; 27 and nothing unclean, and no one who practices abomination and lying, shall ever come into it, but only those whose names are written in the Lamb's book of life."

In that next moment, John was carried away. He found himself upon the New Earth. There he saw the holy city, Jerusalem, coming down out of heaven from God, shining with the glory of God. Her brilliance was like a very valuable gem, like a stone of crystal-clear jasper. The walls of the great and holy city seemed to touch the sky. Along the side were twelve gates. At each gate had a name of one of the twelve tribes of the sons of Israel.

There were three gates on the east, three gates on the north, three gates on the south, and three gates on the west. The wall of the city had twelve foundation stones and on them were the twelve names of the twelve apostles of the Lamb. The one who spoke with gave me a gold measuring rod to measure the city, its gates, and its wall. The city looked as if it was a perfect square. As John measured the city was 1,400 miles in length, width, and height. That would mean that this holy city had two million square miles of space in it. The walls thickness measured, 144 cubits thick in width, which is about 216 feet by human measurement. John looked closely as the material of the wall was jasper and the city was pure gold, like clear glass. "The foundation stones of the city wall were decorated with every kind of precious stone. The first foundation stone was jasper; the second, sapphire; the third, chalcedony; the fourth, emerald; the fifth, sardonyx; the sixth, sardius; the seventh, chrysolite; the eighth, beryl; the ninth, topaz; the tenth, chrysoprase; the eleventh, jacinth; the twelfth, amethyst." Every precious stone seemed to cover the city walls. The twelve gates that sat in the walls of the city were made of a single pearl.

Revelation 22:1-7 "And he showed me a river of the water of life, clear as crystal, coming from the throne of God and of the Lamb, 2 in the middle of its street. On either side of the river was the tree of life, bearing twelve kinds of fruit, yielding its fruit every month; and the leaves of the tree were for the healing of the nations. 3 There will no longer be any curse; and the throne of God and of the Lamb will be in it, and His bond-servants will serve Him; 4 they will see His face, and His name will be on their foreheads. 5 And there will no longer be any night; and they will not have need of the light of a lamp nor the light of the sun, because the Lord God will illuminate them; and they will reign forever and ever. 6 And he said to me, "These words are faithful and true"; and the Lord, the God of the spirits of

the prophets, sent His angel to show His bond-servants
the things which must soon take place.7 "And behold,
I am coming quickly. Blessed is the one who keeps the
words of the prophecy of this book."

As John looked into the mighty city, the street of the city was pure
gold, like transparent glass. John looked and saw no temple in the city,
as was found in the history of the Jews, for the Lord God the Almighty
and the Lamb are its temple.

The glory of God radiated throughout the city. "There was no need
for the sun or of the moon to shine, for the glory of God has illuminated
it, and its lamp is the Lamb."

The river of the water of life, clear as crystal, flowed from the
throne of God and of the Lamb, in the middle of its street. On each side
of the river was the tree of life, bearing twelve kinds of fruit, yielding
its fruit every month.

All of this seems to overwhelm John as he tried to comprehend it.
"There will no longer be any curse; and the throne of God and of the
Lamb will be in it, and His bond-servants will serve Him; they will see
His face, and His name will be on their foreheads. And there will no
longer be any night; and they will not have need of the light of a lamp
nor the light of the sun, because the Lord God will illuminate them;
and they will reign forever and ever."

The angel looked at John and said to him, "These words are faithful
and true"; and the Lord, the God of the spirits of the prophets, sent
His angel to show His bond-servants the things which must soon take
place."

How would you try to describe this city? It is indescribable. It is like trying to describe God. How can human language describe God? By the same measure, how can the human language describe the city where God's presence is centered and where Jesus Christ dwells? This is the problem that John had in trying to describe the New Jerusalem. The words are beyond his comprehension, but he is doing the best he can to describe its glory.

What will the new earth be like? Heaven will not be like our life here on Earth. There will be no disappointments in Heaven. No pain, hurts, temptation, and no sin. Humans have many misconceptions about heaven. Many people picture Heaven as a never-ending church service in the sky.

They imagine that we will sit on fluffy clouds, float in the air, and be continually on our face worshiping God. In fact, Heaven will be glorious and full of grandeur. We will experience the fullness of joy as we live in the presence of God and fellowship with each other. We won't be bored in Heaven, that is a sinful human characteristic. We will not be lonely in Heaven. Most importantly we will have Jesus, but we will also be surrounded by our family and friends who know Jesus as their Savior. We are going to spend eternity with God, with His angels, with the Old Testament saints, and with Christians through all the ages. Can you imagine being in an environment like that? Our relationships will be open, honest, interesting, loving, and uncomplicated by sin or our sinful natures. We will dwell with God, the angels, and one another in perfect compatibility and refreshing intimacy.

Heaven will be an infinite world of new discoveries and Jesus Christ will unfold them to you. This joy will go on increasing forever! It will be so wonderous that we won't even remember what the old Earth was like.

> Isaiah 65:17 "For behold, I create new heavens and a new earth; And the former things will not be remembered or come to mind."

The New Heaven and New Earth will be God resetting and recreating the Heavens and the Earth, where sin and the effects of sin will no longer be present. You will be able to enjoy the beauty of God's presence in all of His glory, unhindered by the presence of sin. The New Earth will be a place of unimaginable beauty and unforetold riches, not for our wealth, but for our enjoyment.

One of the first things you will discover is the beauty of this place. I know in our world we have the stunning beauty of God's creation, but remember all of it is flawed by sin.

Nothing we can see here on this earth will be able to hold a candle to what God has prepared for us. Before sin, the world was perfect. As God described it in Genesis, "it was very good." I believe that God can do nothing less than perfect, so I believe that it will be perfect just as it was in the beginning before sin. The New Earth will have all the beauty of all his creation including animals.

How can I describe to you what Heaven is like? Every word that I describe will be nothing compared to anything on this Earth. Every description that I will try to give you will fail in comparison to the true newness that God has in store for us.

> 2 Corinthians 2:9 "but just as it is written: "things which eye has not seen and ear has not heard, and which have not entered the human heart, all that God has prepared for those who love Him.""

The physical world which God fashioned is the world to which we belong and the one his elect will enjoy and rule for all of eternity.

The new world to come is far more glorious than the one we presently know. However, there are great continuities between this one and the one we long for. It will be a world that we recognize and one in which all the things that we love will be present, but no longer marred and twisted by sin.

We will work for all eternity, but not for the love of or need for money, but for the joy of work. It is also clear from the Bible that we will work in the New Earth. Work was something Adam was made to do: "God took the man and put him in the Garden of Eden to work it and take care of it" (Gen 2:15). Many believe that work is a curse, but the reality is that God made work and it was part of the very good earth before Adam and Eve's fall from grace.

It is only after Adam's sin that work is cursed. It is the curse that makes work often difficult. We will all have a purpose and plan created by God as we enjoy Him for all eternity as we love, laugh, sing and experience a whole new life without sin.

THE FINAL MESSAGE

The words John had heard rung throughout his mind, "And behold, I am coming quickly. Blessed is the one who keeps the words of the prophecy of this book." At this moment John bowed down.

Revelation 22:8-15 "I, John, am the one who heard and saw these things. And when I heard and saw them, I fell down to worship at the feet of the angel who showed me these things. 9 And he said to me, "Do not do that; I am a fellow servant of yours and of your brothers the prophets, and of those who keep the words of this book. Worship God!" 10 And he said to me, "Do not seal up the words of the prophecy of this book, for the time is near. 11 Let the one who does wrong still do wrong, and the one who is filthy still be filthy; and let the one who is righteous still practice righteousness, and the one who is holy still keep himself holy."12 "Behold, I am coming quickly, and My reward is with Me, to reward each one as his work deserves. 13 I am the Alpha and the Omega, the first and the last, the beginning and the end."14 Blessed are those who wash their robes, so that they will have the right to the tree of life, and may enter the city by the gates. 15 Outside are the dogs, the sorcerers, the sexually immoral persons, the murderers, the idolaters, and everyone who loves and practices lying." 16 "I, Jesus, have sent My angel to testify to you of these things for the churches. I am the root and the descendant of David, the bright morning star." 17 The Spirit and the bride say, "Come." And let the one who hears say, "Come." And let the one who is thirsty come; let the one who desires, take the water of life without cost.18 I testify to everyone who hears the words of the prophecy of this book: if anyone adds to them, God will add to him the plagues that are written in this book; 19 and if anyone takes away from the words of the book of this prophecy, God will take away his part from the tree of life and from the holy city, which are written in this book. 20 He who testifies to these things says, "Yes, I am coming quickly." Amen. Come, Lord Jesus. 21 The grace of the Lord Jesus be with all. Amen."

John could not stand at the moment. He heard these words but fell in a position of worship. "I fell down to worship at the feet of the angel who showed me these things. In an instant, the angel said, "Do not do that; I am a fellow servant of yours and of your brothers the prophets, and of those who keep the words of this book. Worship God!" John was told, "Do not seal up the words of the prophecy of this book, for the time is near. Let the one who does wrong still do wrong, and the one who is filthy still be filthy; and let the one who is righteous still practice righteousness, and the one who is holy still keep himself holy."

This was a message John was to share with everyone. It was one of true repentance from our sins. Jesus is coming back soon, and the treasure of Heaven that He alone holds is with Him.

These final words of Jesus given in the Book of Revelation bring significance to everything that John had seen and heard.

Jesus, who is the Alpha and Omega, the first and the last, the beginning and the end, is in control of the past, the present, and the future. In His time, He will bring all history into completion.

Three times in Revelation 22 Jesus says, "I am coming quickly." The fact is Jesus is coming soon. We do not know when that day will be, but we do know that when He comes, these events which we see pictured here in Revelation are going to happen quickly.

The Lord's return can happen at any minute; therefore, we are called not to be careless, but to always be prepared for the moment of His coming.

There is genuine danger in failing to pay attention to the warnings of the Living God. When someone ignores His warning, they are gambling with far more than comfort, they are gambling with eternal damnation, and that is a cost from which none can ever recover. Are you ready? Are you living in light of His return?

CONCLUSION

Where are you at in your life? Have you trusted Jesus Christ as your Savior? Have you confessed your sins and asked Jesus for forgiveness?

We have seen the redemption of Jesus Christ and the future that is in store for those who have put their faith in Jesus Christ and the future of those who do not. The choice is yours. God never sends anyone to hell. We make the choice. Will you choose the free gift of God's salvation or will you not, and perish forever in hell?

When Jesus died on the cross, he said three words, "It is finished" (John 19:30). It was on the cross that Jesus overcame sin's grip. It was there that he canceled sin's debt. As we see, the resurrection broke death's power but only after the debt was paid for on the cross.

Where will you go when you die? If you do not know, then today is the day. Do not say you will do it tomorrow, for tomorrow may never come.

We are all sinners, which means we all have done wrong in our life. Romans 3:23 "for all have sinned and fall short of the glory of God,"

We are born with sin and we all personally choose to sin. Sin is what makes us unsaved. Sin is what separates us from God. Sin is what has us on the path to eternal destruction.

The way you can be saved from the wrath of God and Hell is to. "Believe in the Lord Jesus, and you will be saved". (Acts 13:31)

God has already done all of the work. All you must do is receive, in faith, the salvation God offers. Fully trust in Jesus alone as the payment for your sins.

Believe in Him, and you will not perish. Ask for forgiveness of your sins. God is offering you salvation as a gift. All you have to do is accept it. Jesus is the way of salvation. John 14:6 "Jesus said to him, "I am the way, and the truth, and the life; no one comes to the Father except through Me."

> **John 3:16-17 "For God so loved the world, that He gave His only Son, so that everyone who believes in Him will not perish, but have eternal life. 17 For God did not send the Son into the world to judge the world, but so that the world might be saved through Him.**

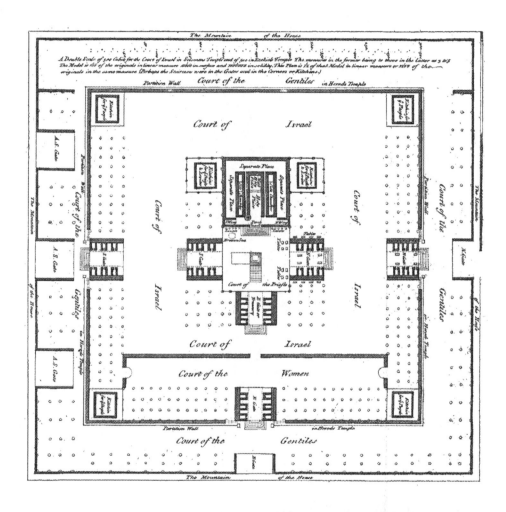

ENDNOTES

1 The Temple Chapter 10 The Two Witness and the Holy City
   Revelation 11

Printed in the United States
by Baker & Taylor Publisher Services